ideabook
for
teaching
design

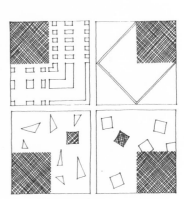

This book is dedicated to everyone who has been,
is, or will be a design student

ideabook
for
teaching
design

moura quayle
University of British Columbia

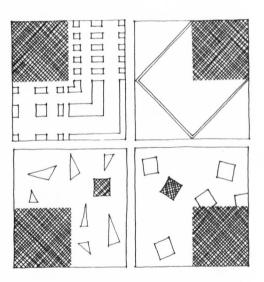

PDA Publishers Corporation
Mesa, Arizona

Library of Congress Cataloging in Publication Data

Quayle, Moura, 1951-
   Ideabook for teaching design.

   Bibliography: p.
   Includes index.
   1. Architectural design--Study and teaching.
I. Title.
NA2750.Q39 1985   729'.07   84-25575
ISBN 0-914886-28-2

PDA PUBLISHERS CORPORATION
1725 East Fountain
Mesa, Arizona 85203-5121

contents

preface

The **Ideabook** responds to the lack of accessible information on techniques for teaching design. It is a workbook that design teachers can use for scribbling inspirational additions, crossing out contentious points and thoughtfully noting questions. The **Ideabook** has the potential to be the beginning of an idea exchange system among design teachers.

In the process of researching and writing the **Ideabook** I had these main concerns:

1. Design teachers are rarely trained as educators;

2. Design teachers overextend themselves by trying to function 100 percent as practitioners, researchers **and** educators;

3. Design teachers have profound positive and negative effects on design students and therefore on the design professions.

The **Ideabook** responds to these concerns by pointing teachers to background information on education theories and processes, by presenting the information in an easy to use reference format and by raising issues about how powerful teachers are and the enormous responsibilities that come with that power.

I hope that design teachers will use and enjoy this book.

1. INTRODUCTION

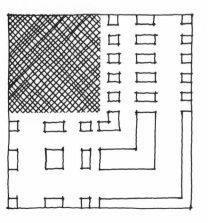

A. PURPOSE OF IDEABOOK

The purpose of a book of ideas for teaching design is to improve teaching and learning design by making good information about teaching techniques accessible. By design, I mean the process of developing appropriate physical solutions in response to specific needs of people and the environment. The following disciplines design in this basic sense: landscape architects, architects, planners, engineers, industrial designers and interior designers. They may find this **Ideabook** useful. By design studios, I mean the various formats that are possible for teaching the above disciplines.

Why this kind of Ideabook? Teaching and learning design in a studio, lecture, seminar or community workshop should be stimulating and enjoyable. This potential for excitement and learning is seldom attained. There is a lack of easily accessible information on education generally, and teaching design in specific, usable by design teachers who are "visual" people, too busy or not motivated to read extensive literature on the subject. This information is of two types: the substance of **what** to teach (theories, design knowledge, etc.) and the ways or **techniques** for teaching. It is NOT the intention of the **Ideabook** to address the substance of design education or what we teach. It is instead a "how-to" book concentrating on practical ideas and techniques that are valuable to design teachers -- regardless of the design theories they espouse or what they teach. Form and content are difficult to separate. A parallel **Ideabook** investigating what to teach is also a much needed document.

The **Ideabook** is intended to fill the information gap by providing ideas about teaching that are:

1. practical and usable;

2. easy to digest;

3. inspirational to spark even better and more personal ideas;

4. set out like yellow pages for searching out teaching information, especially helpful literature.

By improving the teaching and learning of design professions, we are improving the quality of the professions. If students leave school well motivated, competent and energetic about their profession and still eager to learn, teachers have done their job well.

Accessible information on the how's, not the what's, of teaching will allow much more than a basic "seat of the pants" approach -- the method all two popular in the past. The responsibility of teaching is too great and the stakes too high to expect students to continue accepting unprepared teachers.

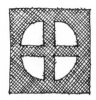

B. DEFINITION OF TERMS

The following terms, because of their frequent use, require definition in the context of the **Ideabook.**

1. DESIGN is the process of developing appropriate physical solutions in response to specific needs of people and the environment.

2. DESIGN STUDIO is the format chosen to teach design, including the traditional drafting spaces, lecture halls, seminar rooms, the front plaza, the community center, the main street, the regional park or the creekside.

3. TEACHING is the act of helping people learn.

4. EDUCATIONAL IDEOLOGIES are value or belief systems that relate to the nature and conduct of schooling.

5. IDEAS are thoughts or conceptions that reflect an opinion, conviction or principle and which are specific for the stimulation of the imagination and of learning.

C. APPROACH

The approach to gathering information for the **Ideabook** is simple and direct. The quest was for practical suggestions and ideas about design teaching techniques, as well as for a better understanding of the field of education: philosophy, psychology and education theory. A series of interviews with a literature review provided background data. The **Ideabook** developed into four main segments.

Short Cuts reviews key ideas and references helpful to design teachers.

Ideas That Work is organized under keyword headings: Organizing and Preparing; Showing and Telling; Responding; and Projects. The various ideas are then listed under secondary keywords or phrases, as noted in the introduction to Chapter 3.

The chapter sequence is designed to report on the results of the "idea" search. Chapter 2: **Short Cuts** reviews key ideas and literature in the fields of philosophy, psychology and education. Chapter 3: **Ideas That Work** is a compilation of ideas for design teaching techniques from interviews and literature. Chapter 4: **Big Ideas** is a forum for discussing the ideas from Chapters 2 and 3 in relation to design education.

Who will use the Ideabook? This project is intended to assist the novice, the professional and the more experienced instructor in teaching. The **Ideabook** gives the beginning teacher some basic formats and ideas to build on. It will also help a practitioner who brings his/her skills and practical experience to academia through a part-time instructor position. Instead of relying only on their own studio experience of years back, the **Ideabook** brings them up-to-date and provides some basics of teaching that might ordinarily have been overlooked in the busy life of working and teaching. Finally, perhaps the experienced teacher will glance at the book -- to smile at some ideas, agree with others and perhaps find one or two that bear consideration of a new approach.

How do you use the Ideabook? It is arranged with a keyword contents system, with the potential for a more extensive keyword program on a version of the **Ideabook** established on a computerized format. It is organized, not to be read from cover to cover, but to be "idea specific" as a reference manual. For example, if a teacher needs ideas about "telling" this section can be easily found as can literature pertaining to the keyword. This system is operable with a hard copy of the **Ideabook** but will be even more useful eventually on a computer system with an **Ideabook** program. As a reference manual, **Ideabook** can be used regularly, although perhaps it will be of more use in the organization/preparation phase of teaching.

The first source of the **Ideas That Work** were interviews. Some thirty design instructors, from Vancouver to Los Angeles, were chosen for interviews through nomination by professors and students. The instructors are from a variety of design disciplines and geographic locations as indicated by the list in the acknowledgments. A letter was sent to fifty nominees and a follow-up phone call determined an interview date, if available. A structured interview was designed and administered to each instructor on the list. The interviews were taped for reference, but note-taking was the main recording method. On completion of the interview, specific ideas were extracted, input into the computer and assigned keywords. Approximately 140 ideas resulted from all the interviews.

The second source of ideas was a current literature review. Applicable material was researched in the fields of sociology, psychology, education and design. The standard library search procedures were carried out in the University of California, Berkeley library system. Fugitive literature was discovered through interviews, in bibliographies of current literature and in proceedings from conferences.

The ideas range in effectiveness or usefulness depending on the individual teacher. Five people concerned with teaching and learning design have reviewed the ideas and depending on the degree of usefulness the highest rated have been included in the **Ideabook**.

Big Ideas is a personal commentary on the **Ideabook** including an analysis of the ideas from Chapters 2 and 3 and a section on "What Next?" or future directions.

The **Annotated Bibliography** is the list of literature used for the **Ideabook** and deemed helpful to a teacher of design.

The **Ideabook** is but a beginning to a potentially limitless project of recording ideas for teaching design.

2. SHORT CUTS

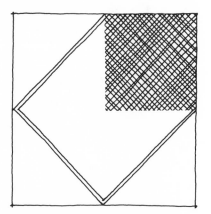

SHORT CUTS

Short Cuts is designed to inform readers of key ideas in the broad fields of philosophy, psychology and education and to guide them to the most valuable references on each subject should they desire more information. The introduction to each general heading evaluates the use of these theories to the design teacher. A brief summary of historical and contemporary theories is found under sub-headings. The best reference and suggested readings are cited; the former is often annotated in more detail suggesting chapters and pages of interest.

The following is a chapter outline:

A. PHILOSOPHY

   i.   educational philosophy
   ii. educational ideology
   iii. teaching modes and roles

B. PSYCHOLOGY

   i.   developmental psychology
   ii. learning theories
   iii. group dynamics
   iv. principles for instruction
   v.   teaching objectives
   vi. educational counseling

C. TECHNIQUES AND METHODS

   i.   teaching techniques
   ii. teaching thinking
   iii. communication

D. PROFESSIONAL/DESIGN EDUCATION

   i.   issues in professional education
   ii. design knowledge
   iii. development of design theories

A. PHILOSOPHY

i. educational philosophy
ii. educational ideology
iii. teaching modes and roles

Knowledge about philosophical systems is a good background for understanding our own beliefs and values. Design education especially, involves discovering and discussing our beliefs and purposes in society. A design teacher must identify a philosophical basis to both a design and a teaching approach. In the same way educational philosophy has grown out of philosophical systems, design philosophy, too, has the same origins. For example, Josuck Koh has compared two design approaches.[1] The first is "reductionistic environmental design"; the major design criteria are internal value systems of a profession. The philosophical orientation, according to Koh, is reductionism/determinism -- meaning the environment is reducible down to "basic elements" and that it can be objectively described and scientifically evaluated so

> 'good' environments or design solutions could be 'rationally' perscribed by designers independent of users' personal, social and cultural variations.[2]

The second approach is "holistic ecological design"; the major design criteria are based on relevance to pressing social problems. The philosophical orientation is realism/holism which is characterized by

> a holistic view of the human-environment system and by an evolutionary and open-ended view of culture and of design and building.[3]

This orientation reflects an intellectual and ethical shift to a holistic, systemic and expansionist view. Koh maintains we are in the process of a paradigm shift from reductionism to holism. (This concept of "shift" will be analyzed in Chapter 4.) Koh's models originate in basic philosophical systems and can be linked to educational ideologies. Using O'Neill's models (see Section A:ii) if you espouse reductionism, the "best fit" educational ideology is liberalism where knowledge is a tool for practical problem solving, based on rational scientific methods. If you espouse holism, then educational liberationism "fits" -- where knowledge is a tool for bringing about social reform. By being aware of these bases for designing and teaching, beginning teachers can evolve and define their own design philosophy and educational ideologies out of which come teaching modes and roles.

The following pages briefly summarize some key ideas in philosophy as applied to education.

i. educational philosophy

Definition: Philosophy can be defined as a "set of coherent generalizations which allow a person to organize his/her overall behavior both systematically and with a minimum of inconsistency and self-contradiction" (William O'Neill, p. 6). The ability to formulate a philosophy is the most systematic development of human reason.

Three Approaches: Educational philosophy has traditionally been approached in three ways:

1. PROBLEM ANALYSIS: Emphasis is on "doing philosophy" in an analytical sense e.g., semantic analysis or what does it mean?

2. FORMAL SYSTEMS APPROACH: Involves basic systems of philosophy like realism or idealism being applied to education.

3. SELF-CONTAINED EDUCATIONAL PHILOSOPHIES: Exist apart from other types of philosophy and are usually based on social ethics. They focus on the relationship of school and society and the implications to the nature and structure of instruction.

Four Educational Philosophical Systems: As taken from Theodore Brameld whose schema are the best known in education circles.

1. PERENNIALISM (classical tradition) seeks absolute standards . . . espoused by Plato and Aristotle.

2. ESSENTIALISM (realism and idealism) represents the ideals of cultural conservation of classical Renaissance humanists.

3. PROGRESSIVISM (pragmatism) makes students into effective problem solvers in the liberal American tradition.

4. RECONSTRUCTIVISM (sociology of knowledge) believes that thinking is a product of living in a particular time . . . espoused by Marx and Mannheim.

 BEST REFERENCE: **Educational Ideologies** by
    William O'Neill

SUGGESTED READINGS: **Patterns of Educational
    Philosophy** by Theodore Brameld

Introduction to Philosophy of Education
    by George F. Kneller

ii. educational ideology

Definition: Educational Ideologies are value or belief systems that relate to the nature and conduct of schooling.

O'Neill's Model: The educational ideologies in O'Neill's model derive from six basic systems of social ethics that are refracted through their corresponding political philosophies to emerge as educational ideologies.

1. EDUCATIONAL FUNDAMENTALISM advocates the revival and affirmation of older and better ways grounded in the uncritical acceptance of "revealed truth" e.g., Hitler or the Moral Majority.

2. EDUCATIONAL INTELLECTUALISM seeks to change practices until they conform to an established rigid intellectual or spiritual ideal e.g., Catholicism or British Public School System.

3. EDUCATIONAL CONSERVATISM wants to preserve and transmit established social patterns to emphasize learning within present day social context e.g., Billy Graham or W. F. Buckley.

4. EDUCATIONAL LIBERALISM advocates preservation and improvement of the existing social order by teaching students to deal with their own emerging life problems e.g., Montessori, Dewey or Piaget.

5. EDUCATIONAL LIBERATIONISM seeks immediate large-scale reform of the established political order to increase freedom and maximize personal potential e.g., women's rights, Skinner, Freire.

6. EDUCATIONAL ANARCHISM supports an open system of experimental inquiry by suggesting the elimination of the existing school system as part of the de-institutionalization process e.g., Illich, Goodman

BEST REFERENCE: **Educational Ideologies** by
   William O'Neill

SUGGESTED READINGS: **Ideology and Education** by
   Richard Pratt

   Contemporary Political Ideologies by L. T.
   Sargent

   JAE: "Politics in the Architecture Studio" by
   Peter Burgess

educational ideology comparison

O'Neill: p. 301-309

	fundamentalism	intellectualism	conservatism	liberalism	liberationism	anarchism
overall goal of education	revive and re-affirm older, better ways	identify, pre-serve & transmit TRUTH	continue established social patterns	promote effective personal behavior	encourage social reforms, personal freedom	eliminate compulsory schooling
objectives of university	encourage return to orig-inal purposes	teach students how to reason	transmit info and skills	teach problem-solving process	respond to need for social reform	self-directed learning
general characteristics	strong moral code; anti-intellect	knowledge as an end in itself	knowledge for social utility	knowledge as a tool for solving problems	knowledge to bring about social reform	knowledge as a product of daily living
student as learner	students are predisposed to error	students are wise and virtuous	students require firm guidance	students on-going behavior is good	within rational society students are good	students are all individuals with different needs
control issues	authority in trained academic managers	authority in educated intellectual elite	authority in responsible educator	authority in trained educator in critical inquiry	authority in enlightened minority	authority returned to "the people"
curriculum subject matter	moral and practical academics	intellectual discipline "the classics"	the 3 r's basic skills	personal effectiveness; explore issues	identity, values and beliefs	free personal choice
methods and evaluation	traditional grading and competition	Socratic questioning; essay exams	compromise between traditional & progressive	open class-rooms, evaluations on simulations	equal emphasis on problem solving & perceiving	self-evaluation

EDUCATIONAL IDEOLOGIES
William O'Neill

O'Neill explores new ways to think about philosophy of education. He uses the term "educational ideologies," meaning value or belief systems that relate to the nature and conduct of schooling, in preference to educational philosophies because it is less academic or abstract. An ideology suggests a specific and dynamic pattern of ideas which in turn can direct social action. O'Neill derives six educational ideologies and describes their origins and characteristics in great detail.

Recommended Reading:

Chapter II: Educational Philosophies and Ideologies (pp. 6-47) NOTE: charts on pp. 30-43

Chapter III: Educational Ideologies . . . An Overview (pp. 48-110); NOTE: p. 54 varying concepts of self; See Ideology Chart on the following page; Try the Educational Ideologies Inventory, p. xxiii

educational ideology tree   O'Neill: p. 61

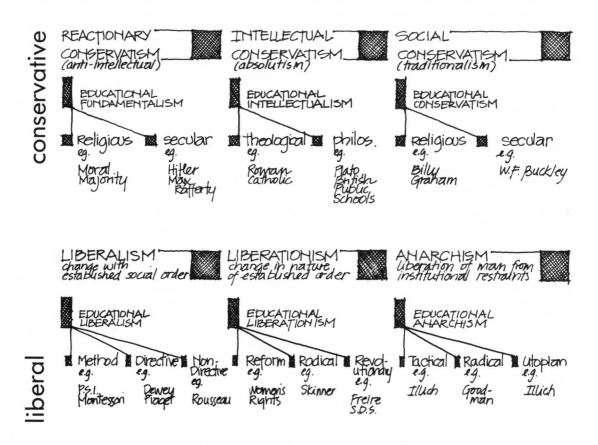

iii. teaching modes and roles

Definition: Teaching modes or orientations are the "way" a teacher says or does things -- their total approach to their craft. Teacher roles are more specific to the methods used or to the desired teaching/learning outcomes.

Four Modes: Four general orientations can be identified:

1. PRINCIPLES AND FACTS ("I teach what I know"): The teacher identifies with the discipline rather than the teaching role . . . there is an emphasis on systematic coverage by lecture (educational intellectualism).

2. INSTRUCTOR-CENTERED ("I teach what I am"): The teacher has a strong ego, radiates self-confidence with an emphasis on teacher dominance in the classroom (educational conservatism).

3. STUDENT AS MIND ("I train minds"): Students are regarded as self-reliant individuals; the teacher emphasizes students' analytical and problem-solving abilities (educational liberalism).

4. STUDENT AS PERSON ("I work with students as people"): The teacher's image is that of counselor and resource person with students viewed as individuals accepting responsibility for their behavior (educational liberationism).

Six Roles:

1. The EXPERT transmits factual information, concepts and perspectives . . . e.g., lecture on site analysis techniques.

2. The FORMAL AUTHORITY sets goals and procedures by defining structure, evaluating performance . . . e.g., grading (A, B, C, etc.).

3. The SOCIALIZING AGENT clarifies goals and career paths to prepare students for the future demands of their professional and personal lives . . . e.g., advising and counseling.

4. The FACILITATOR promotes creativity and growth to help overcome learning obstacles . . . e.g., the in-studio process.

5. The EGO IDEAL demonstrates the ultimate worth of personal commitment to material or educational goals . . . e.g., critiques using teacher's experience.

6. The PERSON conveys the full range of human needs and skills by being self-revealing, trustworthy, warm and open . . . e.g., counseling or just being available to listen and talk.

BEST REFERENCE: **University Teacher as Artist**
Joseph Axelrod

SUGGESTED READINGS: **Improving Teaching Styles**
edited by Kenneth Eble

UNIVERSITY TEACHER AS ARTIST
Joseph Axelrod

Axelrod divides teachers into two groups, those who use didactic methods (employed by teacher-craftsmen) and those who use evocative methods (employed by teacher-artists). The didactic mode stresses either cognitive knowledge acquired primarily by memorization, or mastery of skills acquired by repetition and practice. In the evocative mode the major learning process method is inquiry and discovery. Teachers, on purpose or by default, follow a teaching orientation. The four teaching prototypes suggested by Axelrod are examples of models showing attitudes of teachers towards themselves, their students and towards teaching and learning in general. By examining these generic approaches, beginning teachers may gain insight into what orientation is appropriate for them. The most interesting aspect of **University Teacher as Artist** is the use of transcripts of actual class sessions which allow the reader to observe evocative teacher-artists at work.

Recommended Reading:

Part One: **The Art of University Teaching** (pp. 5-55)
    Chapter 1: Didactic and Evocative Teaching Modes
    Chapter 2: Portraits of Evocative Teachers
    Chapter 3: Distinguishing Features in the
        Portraits

Part Two: **Portrait of a Teacher Artists** (pp. 57-144)
    Chapter 4: Before Berkeley: Teaching Books
    Chapter 5: Late Sixties: Training Minds
    Chapter 6: Early Seventies: Working with Students
        as People

B. PSYCHOLOGY

    i. developmental psychology
    ii. learning theories
    iii. group dynamics
    iv. principles for instruction
    v. teaching objectives
    vi. educational counseling

Developmental Psychology: Knowledge of developmental psychology is basic to teaching any discipline. Identifying the intellectual and personality factors that students bring with them as they engage in learning allows application of that knowledge to teaching and curriculum structure.

Randy Pierce and Mike Martin of Kansas State University [4] conducted an investigation to explore the connection between the developmental characteristics of beginning design students and Piaget's and Maslow's theories (see section B:i). The research focused on two question: (1) In terms of intelligence and need/motivation, what are the developmental characteristics of design and non-design majors? (2) If there are changes in the developmental characteristics of students, can we attribute any of that change specifically to environmental design education? For specific results of the study refer to the 1979 Associated Collegiate Schools of Architecture (ACSA) paper.[5]

Pierce and Martin suggest the following scenarios to explain the connection between Piaget's stages of Intellectual Growth and design learning tasks. A prerequisite in the learner of CONCRETE OPERATIONS (ability to process real information) is necessary to perform this task properly . . .

    a graphics instructor discusses verbally and illustrates the concept of 'picture plane' by employing a piece of plexiglass and two cardboard cubes.

Another scenario suggests a prerequisite of FORMAL OPERATIONS (ability to process abstract information) . . .

    a design instructor has students identify, classify and interrelate data into an organized structure consisting of such concepts as local site and climate conditions, circulation, economic base, lifestyle and then discuss the possible implications of these concepts in shaping the form of future physical environments.

The observations and acknowledgment of students at various stages allows teachers to fine tune their instructional objectives and the kind of projects they assign.

The following scenarios connect Maslow's theories to design learning situations. Students come to learning situations with a variety of needs and motivations. The student with high security needs is concerned with immediate and future safety. This scenario reflects students' need for security . . .

a student feels the instructor should follow the book and only put a little variation or added material into a lecture.

Esteem needs often stand between the student and intellectual curiosity. The next scenario illustrates the process of gratifying esteem needs . . .

In the design studio, the professor offers the solution to a design problem for a student, and the student didn't like this. She said she would have liked to resolve the situation herself even though it would be hard work and time consuming.

In conclusion Pierce and Martin emphasize that an understanding of students' developmental character is essential if educators hope to respond to the richness and diversity of people. "Design education must become a vehicle through which the students gain a capacity for life-long renewal."[6]

Learning Theories: Knowledge of learning theories means the design teacher has the background information to perscribe to some synthesized theory and use this approach to write instructional objectives and to evaluate processes of learning in various studio situations. For instance, Ray Lifchez (professor of architecture at the University of California, Berkeley) makes use of such learning concepts in his introductory environmental design studio. From a participant/observer position, he is practicing teaching that emphasizes reflection or exploratory understanding. Reflective teaching and learning is problem-centered and involves exploratory personal involvement. The underlying learning theory is cognitive field theory, where learners are "situationally and perceptually" active. Lifchez uses various techniques to help students discover contradictions or inconsistencies in their thinking -- which is part of reflective teaching and learning. Bigge outlines these techniques generally[7] and Lifchez's examples make the connection to design education. Bigge's "context switch" is reflected in the studio project by moving from small scale to large scale (1/4 to 1/2 scale). This way students see the project in a new light. Bigge's "introduction of disturbing data" is manifested by Lifchez in the adding of new issues to the inquiry underway in the studio problem.

Objectives: Both principles of and objectives for instruction have obvious application to teaching design. They form the basis for decision making on course outlines and objectives. Every course is as successful as the clarity and realistic qualities of the course objectives. Too often in design studios there appear to be no defined objectives. This leaves most people confused through the process with no sense of accomplishment at the end. Teachers must prepare course objectives and communicate them to students.

Group Dynamics and Educational Counseling: Knowledge of group dynamics and educational counseling is invaluable for a design teacher. The studio "group" is always unique but generally follows basic theories. These dynamics are influential on the teaching/learning environment in that they can either facilitate or block communication among the group participants -- teacher/ resource person and the students. Counseling is part of the role of teacher as socializing agent and teacher as person. Teachers prepare students for future demands of professional and personal life and convey the range of human qualities in listening to and counseling students.

17

The following pages briefly summarize some key theories in psychology as applied to education. The reader is referred to the bibliography for complete citations of the best references and suggested readings.

the ideological designer

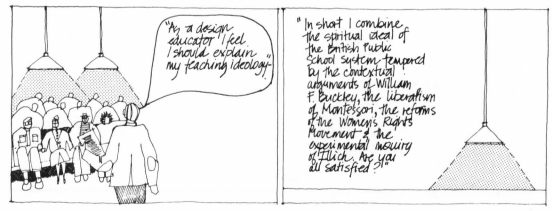

i. cognitive - developmental psychology

Piaget's Model: Jean Piaget began his studies of cognitive development in Paris over 50 years ago. Piaget's model of the development of the intellect emphasizes that operations of logic are learned through an interaction of problems calling for the operations in a non-verbal context. Piaget's work over the years has resulted in a clear delineation of learning and a description of the sequence of cognitive or intellectual development in the human species.

Piaget's Terminology evolved as he attempted to interpret his observations of children and thus postulate a theory. A reflex SCHEMA is an innate mental organization that becomes stabilized with repeated activations brought about by motor activity and sensory perceptions. To Piaget, intelligence is the dynamic process by which experience extends the existing mental organization -- thus making the person more ADAPTIVE.

Piaget's Stages of Intellectual Growth: A three stage classification is summarized here:

I. SENSORI-MOTOR DEVELOPMENT (birth to 2 years): The child moves from undifferentiated reflexive activity through intermediate adaption stages to objective representation of relation between parts of the physical world. The preverbal stage is characterized by cognitive operations such as eye-hand coordination while the pre-operational representation stage is characterized by the appearance of symbolic and intuitive thought -- making use of language -- which finds expression in symbolic play.

II. CONCRETE OPERATIONS (2-11 years): The child learns to handle language which is used for egocentric and social ends as well as a means of representing relationships in the physical world. The individual can perform internal manipulations of data, e.g., number, classification and seriation; the information must be real and/or perceivable, not purely verbal or abstract.

III. FORMAL OPERATIONS (11-15 years): During this stage of cognitive development the youth learns to use language to think about abstract ideas. Concrete operations are surpassed as the individual develops the capacity of formal, propositional thinking. He/she can distinguish the form from the content of a statement and consider the reasoning aside from the specific content.

BEST REFERENCE: **Psychological Foundations of Learning and Teaching** by Wilson, Robeck, and Michael

SUGGESTED READING: **Essentials of Learning** by Robert Travers

i. emotional - developmental psychology

Freud's Model: According to Freud, libidinal energy is the driving force behind all human activity. Opposed to this drive is a resistance that causes regression to less complicated states of existence. The strengths of these two forces determines the developmental phases of an individual. These Freudian concepts are based on punishment avoidance rather than reward or reinforcement.

Summary of Freudian Stages:

1. ORAL (birth-18 months: Earliest contact with the world is through mouth . . .

2. ANAL (18 months-4 years): Sensual sensitivities shift from mouth to anus . . . independence through locomotion.

3. PHALLIC (3-5 years): Sensual satisfactions from attention to genitals . . . the Oedipus complex emerges.

4. LATENT (elementary school): Sexual urges reduced or quiescent.

5. PUBERTAL: Instinctual forces move individual to choose love object.

Freud conceptualized the possibility of regression to one of these early stages under condition of threat or aggression.

Erikson's Model: Erikson, trained in Germany, emmigrated to America and carried forward some basic Freudian principles. He maintained that the various stages of development are a series of characteristic crises in psychological life that are resolved for healthy growth. Erikson's ideas emphasize the power of cultural influences over instinctual forces.

Summary of Erikson's Stages: These stages describe the ego qualities which emerge from critical periods of development.

1. Development of a sense of trust -- emotional patterns are set during this period (oral).

2. Developing a sense of autonomy -- function of ego, development of holding and letting go (anal).

3. Locomotor/genital age . . . sense of initiative acquired (phallic).

4. Age 6-12 . . . acquiring a sense of industry, building self-image, skill building, warding off sense of inferiority.

5. Early adolescent . . . sense of identity . . . warding off identity diffusion or not knowing who you are.

6. Young adulthood . . . acquires a sense of intimacy and solidarity . . . selection of mate and of occupational pattern.

7. Young married . . . acquires a sense of generativity.

8. Adult development . . . acquires a sense of integrity and avoids a sense of despair.

 BEST REFERENCE: **Psychological Foundations of Learning and Teaching** by Wilson, Robeck and Michael

SUGGESTED READINGS: **Contemporary Theories and Systems in Psychology** by B. Wolman

the emotional designer

i. personality - developmental psychology

Maslow's Theories of motivation and personality focus on the affective domain of human development. Maslow believes man has a number of primary, instinctive motives like hunger to the higher motive for self-actualization. The "lower" the motive the more crucial it is for survival.

PHYSIOLOGICAL NEEDS . . . The strongest and the most critical of our needs and therefore the first on the hierarchy . . . quest for nourishment, good health and shelter from the elements.

SECURITY NEEDS . . . if the physiological needs are met then the needs for security and safety emerge . . . efforts to satisfy these needs are clearly expressed in young children and neurotic adults.

BELONGINGNESS NEEDS . . . the next set of motives emerge with the needs for love and belongingness as the person yearns for a friend, a companion, a lover and a place in a group.

ESTEEM NEEDS . . . self-esteem and esteem-from-others becomes important when a person feels loved. The individual seeks respect from themself and from others.

SELF-ACTUALIZATION . . . this is the highest level of Maslow's need hierarchy -- the seeking of self-fulfillment and the becoming all one can be.

BEST REFERENCE: **Towards the Psychology of Being**
by Abraham Maslow

PSYCHOLOGICAL FOUNDATIONS OF LEARNING AND TEACHING
John A. R. Wilson, Mildred C. Robeck, William B. Michael

Based on the research findings (1974) **PSYCHOLOGICAL FOUNDATIONS** provides the tools to aid teachers in using learning and human development theory to help students become "self-directing" individuals. Central to this book is a learning/motivation model which is a thread tying all the information together. This model integrates research findings about conditioned response learning, conceptual insight, and motivational dimensions of behavior. A learning/motivation theory shows interaction between cognitive learning and emotions at three levels:

a. ASSOCIATION LEARNING: Facts and details, accepted and stored;

b. CONCEPTUALIZATION: Material is organized, inherent meanings and structures are discovered;

c. CREATIVE SELF DIRECTION: Students uses ideas and knowledge to create something new.

The student's thinking process determines his/her level of learning rather than the content of the subject matter.

Recommended Reading:

CHAPTER 2: Perspective on Learning and Motivation
   (pp. 15-42);
CHAPTER 5: Affective Associations (pp. 101-130)
CHAPTER 10: Personality and Social Learning (pp.
   47-274)
CHAPTER 12: Development of Perceptual Abilities (pp.
   307-326)
CHAPTER 13: Emotional Development (pp. 327-350)
CHAPTER 14: Cognitive Growth: Piaget's Theory (pp.
   351-384)

the needy designer

ii. learning theories

Definition: A learning theory is a systematic, integrated outlook on how people relate to their environment and enhance their ability to use both themselves and their environments more effectively (Bigge p. 3). Psychology is a field characterized by several schools of thought; learning theories are ascribed to many of these schools.

Two families: Twentieth century systematic learning theories may be classified into two broad families: behavioristic and Gestalt field.

A. In STIMULUS-RESPONSE (S-R) CONDITIONING THEORIES of the BEHAVIORISTIC family **learning is a change in observable behavior** which occurs through stimuli and responses becoming related according to mechanistic principles. Proponents are B. F. Skinner and R. M. Gagne.

B. In COGNITIVE THEORIES of the GESTALT-FIELD family **learning is a process of gaining or changing insights**, outlooks, expectations, or thought patterns. These theories use **person** instead of organism, **interaction** instead of action or reaction and **psychological environment** instead of biological or physical environment. These concepts enable the teacher to see a person, his/her environment and his/her interaction with that environment as all occurring at once -- this is the meaning of FIELD. Proponents are J. S. Bruner and Rollo May. A behavioristic teacher desires to change observable behavior of students in a significant way; A Gestalt-field oriented teacher aspires to help students change their understandings of problems or situations.

Making a Choice? Teachers may adhere to one position in theory and practice, selectively borrow from conflicting positions to form a mosaic that they draw upon as needed, or develop **emergent syntheses** from their own thoughts on the conflicting theories. The latter becomes a new systematic outlook which benefits from ideas of conflicting approaches but does not form a compromise. Cognitive-Field Learning Theory is an emergent synthesis.

BEST REFERENCE: **Learning Theories for Teachers** by Morris L. Bigge

SUGGESTED READINGS: **Theories of Learning and Instruction** by E. Hilgaard

The Experience of Teaching and Learning by William Adams

Essentials of Learning by Robert Travers

LEARNING THEORIES FOR TEACHERS
Morris L. Bigge, 4th Ed. 1982

This text gives an overall picture of modern learning theories in a readable style. It guides readers in critically constructing and evaluating their approaches regarding the nature of the learning process. Bigge's bias lies with the cognitive-field theory of learning but he has mananged a balanced treatment of learning theories that gives a very useful overview.

Recommended Reading:

Chapter 2: Presents the more prominent representatives of pre-twentieth century learning theory -- a historical background.

Chapters 3 and 4: Introduce the two major contrasting twentieth century families of learning theory -- the stimulus/response conditioning and Gestalt-field theories and give a specific explanation of each.

Chapters 12, 13, 14: Develop the relationships of the various learning theories to teaching practices -- for example Chapter 12 addresses: How is teaching related to learning?

the learning and learned designer

theories of learning

Bigge: p. 10-11

	learning theory	psychological system	basis for learning transfer	emphasis in teaching	key persons	contemporary exponents
mental discipline theories / SUBSTANCE	THEISTIC MENTAL DISCIPLINE	faculty psychology	exercised faculties, automatic transfer	exercise faculties of the mind	St. Augustine, John Calvin	Hebraic Christian fundamentalists
	HUMANISTIC DISCIPLINE	classical humanism	cultivated mind or intellect	training of intrinsic mental power	Plato, Aristotle	M.J. Adler
	SELF-ACTUALIZATION	romantic naturalism	recapitulation of history, no transfer	permissive education centred on feelings	Rousseau, Progressivists	John Holt, A. Maslow
	APPERCEPTION	structuralism	growing apperceptive mass	addition of new mental states to store of old ones	J.F. Herbart	many teachers and administrators
S-R conditioning theories / BEHAVIORISTIC	S-R (stimulus/response) BOND	connectionism	identical elements	promotion of desired S-R connections	E.L. Thorndike	A.I. Gates, J.M. Stephens
	CONDITIONING with no re-inforcement	classical conditioning	conditioned responses & reflexes	promotion of desired responses to appropriate stimuli	J.B. Watson	E.R. Guthrie
	CONDITIONING through re-inforcement	instrumental conditioning	conditioned responses & S-R induction	systematic ew changes, increase probability of desired response	C.L. Hull	B.F. Skinner, R.M. Gagné
cognitive theories / GESTALT FIELD	INSIGHT	gestalt psychology	transposition of generalized insights	promotion of insightful learning	K. Koffka	W. Köhler
	GOAL INSIGHT	configuration-ationism	tested insights	aid students in developing high quality insights	B.H. Bode	E.E. Bayles
	COGNITIVE FIELD	positive relativism	continuity, experience, insights	help students restructure their life spaces	E.C. Tolman, J. Dewey	M.L. Bigge, J.S. Bruner

iii. group dynamics

Kurt Lewin's Theories of Group Dynamics: Lewin applies concepts of the psychology of the individual to group behavior; he feels the group is a unit which has to be analyzed as a whole.

> **1. Analogy between individual and group psychology:** The group and its environment form a social field. The social happening is viewed as occurring and being a result of coexisting social entities -- e.g., groups and subgroups. An important characteristic is the relative position of these entities within a group's field; the forces acting there are decisive factors in a group's behavior.
>
> **2. Issue of Causation:** Lewin considers group behavior as a function of the total situation. The social field at any given time offers the entire interpretation of group behavior.
>
> **3. Dynamic Interdependence:** Groups are characterized by the dynamic interdependence of their members. Any group is exposed to cohesive and disruptive forces -- the latter may result from too strong barriers between group members that hamper communication or from conflict between the individual's goals. Each group is a field of forces.

BEST REFERENCES: **Contemporary Theories and Systems in Psychology** by B. Wolman

SUGGESTED READINGS: **Small Group Teaching** by Shlomo and Yael Sharan

Teaching Social Change: A Group Approach by Zinberg, Boris and Boris

iv. principles of instruction

Ten Selected Principles: The following are principles, based on research evidence, which should be considered in designing teaching activities:

1. PRELEARNING PREPARATION: Learners must have mastered prerequisite behaviors in order to succeed in those behaviors they are required to learn. A preview helps students acquire a "predisposition" towards what is to follow **(review of material learned in previous studio -- quick sketch problem or discussion).**

2. MOTIVATION: Students are more efficient if they have a desire to learn what is being taught. Goals or incentives can be "to know," "to be able to do something related to what is learned in the present or the near future" or "to obtain immediate or future benefits and rewards unrelated to what is learned" (see chart pp. 74-75 Kibler: **Objectives for Instruction and Evaluation) (connect studios "doings" to reality and show how a particular skill is important in the design process).**

3. PROVIDE A MODEL OF TERMINAL PERFORMANCE: Learners should be shown examples of what they are to produce or do at the end of a learning experience **(showing other student work, professional work and your own work).**

4. ACTIVE RESPONDING: Learners can profit from watching or listening to someone else perform the acts to be learned . . . BUT it is what the learner DOES that determines learning **(get students involved in designing and drawing sooner, not later).**

5. GUIDANCE: Learners should be given guidance and prompting when attempting to demonstrate new behaviors that are learned . . . then eliminate prompts gradually **(support and encourage at all levels).**

6. PRACTICE: Opportunities should be provided for learners to use newly learned behaviors repeatedly **(allow opportunities to "redesign" or "redraw").**

7. KNOWLEDGE OF RESULTS: Learner should have prompt and frequent knowledge of the appropriateness or inappropriateness of their responses . . . it is better to provide learner with criteria to evaluate their own responses.

8. GRADUATED SEQUENCE: Subject matter should be organized in hierarchical form from the simple to the complex, from the familiar to the unfamiliar.

9. INDIVIDUAL DIFFERENCES: Learning experience should be designed in such a way that each student may proceed at his or her own pace.

10. TEACHING PERFORMANCE: Various teaching roles require social skills in stimulating interest, explaining, and guiding.

BEST REFERENCE: Objectives for Instruction and Evaluation by Robert Kibler et al.

SUGGESTED READINGS: **Principles of Instructional Design** by Gagne and Briggs

v. instructional objectives

Educational Objectives: Are written at various levels of specificity and for different purposes. **General educational objectives,** non specific, are intended to indicate broad goals of education. **Instructional objectives,** highly specific, are intended to communicate instructional intentions to learners.

Instructional objectives should contain the following elements:

1. WHO is to perform the desired behavior? (e.g., student).

2. The ACTUAL BEHAVIOR to be employed in demonstrating master of the objective . . . e.g., "to draw" -- should be an observable act using action verbs.

3. The RESULT (product or performance) which will be evaluated to determine whether the objective is mastered . . . e.g., "the drawing".

4. The RELEVANT CONDITIONS under which the behavior is to be performed e.g., "two hour charette."

5. The STANDARD that will be used to evaluate the success of the product or performance "specific evaluation criteria for a drawing . . . clarity, line weight, etc."

 BEST REFERENCE: **Preparing Instructional Objectives** by R. Mager

SUGGESTED READING: **Essentials of Learning for Instruction** by R. Gagne

Taxonomy of Educational Objectives by Bloom

Objectives for Instruction and Evaluation by Kibler et al.

PREPARING INSTRUCTIONAL OBJECTIVES
Robert Mager

A course description tells you something about the content and procedures of a course; a course objective describes a desired outcome of a course. Mager's book guides the reader through the preparation process simply and effectively.

Recommended Reading:

the whole book . . . 60 short pages.

OBJECTIVES FOR INSTRUCTION AND EVALUATION
Robert J. Kibler, Donald J. Cegala, Larry L. Barker, David T. Miles

This book represents an effort to identify the important functions that instructional objectives can serve in improving education. According to the authors the book makes the following unique contributions:

1. Information on instructional objectives has been gleaned from a variety of sources.

2. The book illustrates the relationships between instructional or teaching objectives and the teaching/learning process.

3. It prescribes an approach to objectives based on planning instructions and being explicity about instructional goals.

4. It analyzes the elements contained in objectives required to plan instruction.

Recommended Reading:

the objective designer

vi. educational counseling

Stages in the Development of Counseling Methodology:

1. THE DARK AGES: Counseling and theory are non-existent in a professional sense . . .

2. ANALYTICAL PSYCHOLOGY: The legacy of Freud is the importance of early experience, hypnosis, free association and dream interpretation . . .

3. TRAIT AND FACTOR PSYCHOLOGY: Gave us information on appraisal and diagnosis as well as goal setting and evaluation . . .

4. PHENOMENOLOGY: Carl Rogers brought out subjective reality and the sensitive, empathetic client-centered approach . . .

5. LEARNING AND BEHAVIORISM: Demonstrated that special behavior can be changed by simply understanding that behavior is learned . . .

6. EXISTENTIALISM: From Perls came Gestalt Therapy and the client's awareness of reality . . .

 BEST REFERENCE: **Systematic Counseling** by Norman R. Stewart et al.

SUGGESTED READING: **Gestalt Approaches to Counseling** by Allan Dye and Harold Hackney

C. TECHNIQUES & METHODS

i.   teaching techniques
ii. teaching thinking
iii. communication

Teaching techniques and methods are covered well in many "all-purpose" teaching books; the best I found was **Teaching Tips** by Wilbert McKeachie.

Section C:ii "teaching thinking" is most important for design teachers. de Bono's books give a good background to understanding the brain and how it works. For designers, the important kind of thinking is "visual thinking" -- which is a subset of active or generative thinking.

Robert McKim has a section in his book **Experiences in Visual Thinking** on teaching visual thinking (pp. 23-27). He says the first step is to stop "unteaching" it. Opportunities for visual expression decrease drastically after early schooling. Reading, writing and arithmetic detach children from sensory experiences. The one-sided education of the three R's results in "massive visual atrophy." Perceptual loss can be caused by self-consciousness and imaginative loss by parents who scold: "Stop imagining things!" McKim cites three obstacles to be overcome before studying visual thinking: the notion we all see equally well, the apprehension of "no imagination" and the belief that drawing requires rare artistic talent. Design students and teachers should be aware of these obstacles and then create a challenge to be met which can start the visual thinking process.

Designing is communicating. Many of the ideas in Chapter 3 relate to communication. The following literature expands on the techniques of teaching and communicating.

i. teaching techniques

TEACHING TIPS a guidebook for the beginning college teacher
Wilbert J. McKeachie.

Teaching Tips was written to answer the multitude of questions posed by new college teachers, to "place them at ease in their jobs, and to get them started effectively in the classroom" (p. vii). The book covers everything you would ever want to know about teaching -- from detailed ideas about lecturing to a discussion of teacher roles to an A, B, C, of assigning grades.

Recommended Reading:

If you haven't time to read cover to cover (280 easy-to-read pages) concentrate on chapters of interest among the following:

ORGANIZING: Chapter 3: Meeting a class for the first time; Chapter 5: Organizing effective discussions

PREPARING: Chapter 2: Countdown for course preparation; Chapter 23: Motivation, learning and cognition

SHOWING: Chapter 12: Audio-visual techniques; Chapter 13: Role playing and microteaching; Chapter 15: Instructional games, simulations and the case method

TELLING: Chapter 4: Lecturing; Chapter 14: Term papers, student reports, field trips

RESPONDING: Chapter 6: Six roles of teachers; Chapter 19: Counseling and individual instruction; Chapter 27: Improving your teaching

METHODS: Chapter 10: Reading, programmed learning and computer assisted instruction; Chapter 11: PSI, TIPS, contract plans and modular instruction

EVALUATING: Chapter 16: Examinations; Chapter 17: a, b, c's of assigning grades; Chapter 22: Ethical standards in teaching

A checklist of teaching techniques and the goals potentially achieved through their use is found in Appendix C, p. 296.

ii. teaching thinking

Types of Thinking: de Bono's definition of thinking: "Thinking is the deliberate exploration of experience for a purpose" (**Teaching Thinking**, p. 32). He suggests that **critical** thinking (traditional assessment of ideas), **active** thinking (generative, solving problems) and **passive** thinking (scholarly, descriptive, contemplative) all have their place. de Bono is concerned that we not neglect generative thinking which is messy, imperfect, and perhaps more difficult to teach. He emphasizes that thinking should not be a replacement for gut feeling, political identity or commitment: "Emotion is what matters in the end, since it is the final arbiter of human value" (**Teaching Thinking**, p. 20).

de Bono's Tools for Teaching Thinking: de Bono espouses a program for teaching thinking called CORT THINKING (Cognitive Research Trust). The traditional approach is to immerse students in different "thinking" situations and then encourage them to abstract certain principles to be used in other situations. What tends to happen is that the interest and momentum in the content often precludes attention to the thinking process itself. In the CORT approach the "operations" are created deliberately and independently as tools. A thinking situation is then provided for the use and practice of these tools so the students may acquire skill with them. The abstraction process is bypassed. See **Teaching Thinking** for more information.

Wales and Stager . . . Guided Design: Guided design, used in engineering schools, is an instructional approach that emphasizes divergent or open-ended thinking. It utilizes a problem-solving process as the primary tool for integrating the learning of content and problem-solving skills. Students are active learners: they solve problems in groups, learn content by self-instruction (see Stonewater article).

ADAPT program: Approach to instruction in problem solving emphasizes changes in students' cognitive strategies. Analysis of the ADAPT curriculum indicates that students become formal operational thinkers and better critical thinkers. The program is based on Piaget's theory of cognitive growth and emphasizes the concrete and formal learning stages (see Stonewater article).

BEST REFERENCES: **Teaching Thinking** by Edward de Bono

Fostering Critical Thinking, ed. by Robert Young, especially "Can We Really Teach Them to Think?" by Robert Yinger and "Strategies for problem Solving" by Jerry Stonewater

Experiences in Visual Thinking by Robert McKim

iii. communication

Verbal Communication: TALK: consider not just words but volume, tone, pitch and rhythm. There is a whole range of sound intensity between quiet whispers and a pneumatic drill. The rhythm of the voice can be varied by changing speed of delivery, by introducing hesitations, repetitions and silences. Speed of delivery is important -- normal speaking rate is 100-200 words per minute. RECEPTION: hearing does not equal listening. Listening concerns context, identification, interpretation and relationship to existing knowledge. Listening skills are improved by any method involving noticing or questioning things said. Word choices are important -- they convey emotional meanings, prejudice, definitions, fact and habits of thought.

Non-verbal Communication: The three main areas are (1) to support or deny verbal communication, (2) to take the place of verbal communication, and 3) to show emotions and attitudes. For example, eye narrowing generally means the receiver is puzzled or afraid. To avoid threats or being found out people avoid prolonged eye contact. The best advice is that each person should investigate his/her own non-verbal behavior, read up on the subject and engage in self-observation. The non-verbal component in teaching should complement and reinforce the verbal component.

BEST REFERENCE: **Teaching and Learning as a Communication Process** by Philip Hills

SUGGESTED READINGS: **Effective Teaching and Learning** by Otis Lancaster

Learning a Language, Learning to Design by Donald Schon in AES, 1981

the communicative designer

35

D. PROFESSIONAL/DESIGN EDUCATION

i. issues in professional education
ii. design knowledge
iii. development of design theories

The issues in professions today are strongly connected to education. How do we alter the "discontent" identified by Argyris and Schon in Section D:i? Gradually students will exert more influence and will be supported by teachers who have been through the frustrating educational system and are interested in a new model for professional behavior. This will result in students identifying new clients to serve and being guided towards competency that will work for them as professionals.

Design knowledge and the development of design theories relate to the content of the design teaching but they are an integral part of any design education discussion. The issues raised in the following summaries are followed up in more detail in Chapter 4.

i. issues in professional education

Discontent: There is a general "discontent" prevalent in most professions -- the oldest (medicine and law) as well as the relative newcomers such as engineering, business management, architecture and planning. Those who are concerned with professions are also concerned about the education of professionals. Argyris and Schon see five central issues:

1. WHOM DOES THE PROFESSION SERVE? Critics say the professions are not meeting society's needs. Students and young professionals want to serve the disadvantaged and work on social problems but they cannot see any established professional roles that work that way. The advocacy movement has had some success in law but has led to frustration in other fields.

2. ARE PROFESSIONALS COMPETENT? Schools generally fail to help students become competent in practice for the disadvantaged. Instead "the student is expected to acquire competence mysteriously on his own, or by association with extraordinary practitioners" (**Theory in Practice,** p. 143). In general, professional roles are undergoing change.

3. DOES CUMULATIVE LEARNING INFLUENCE PRACTITIONERS? Architecture has little tradition of scholarship and therefore of cumulative learning. A building is a consequence of a theory of some kind -- but the theories are rarely explained and are therefore lost to others because of lack of documentation.

4. IS REFORM POSSIBLE? Three dilemmas exist around reform: (1) The profession tends to be a prisoner of its own world and the professional school is too divorced from the real world of practice -- neither can be counted on to initiate reform; (2) If schools did turn out "new" professionals how would they survive in the professional establishment of the old type? (3) Where are the professionals who will reform professional education? Where is the theory and competence for the practice of reform?

5. CAN SELF-ACTUALIZATION OCCUR? Young professionals want more integration between professional and personal life -- assuring "meaning" in their professional lives.

 BEST REFERENCE: **Theory in Practice** by Argyris and Schon

SUGGESTED READINGS: **Professional Education: New Directions** by Edgar Schein

THEORY IN PRACTICE Increasing professional effectiveness
Chris Argyris and Donald Schon

If we regard deliberate human behavior as the consequence of theories of action, then we explain or predict a person's behavior by attributing such a theory to him or her. According to Argyris and Schon, we each have a set of interrelated theories of action for a specific situation -- called theories of practice. These theories specify the actions that will yield intended consequences. Thus, teachers have a theory of practice which they expect will yield learning on the part of their students. Theories of action are of two types: espoused and theories-in-use. An espoused theory of action is one to which a person gives allegiance and communication to others. A theory-in-use actually governs the action. Too often, the individual may not be aware of incompatibility between espoused theories and theories-in-use. Argyris and Schon argue that there are serious affects on the learning process if there are inconsistencies between our espoused theories and our theories-in-use. They suggest two models under which we operate in personal and professional situations as well as methods for moving from ineffective Model I behavior to the more effective Model II behavior.

Recommended Reading:

The whole book is worthwhile but if time is an issue
    concentrate on:

Part I: Theory (pp. 3-20)
Part II: Action . . . Chapter 3: Diagnosing Theories in
    Use
Charts: Model I (p. 68) and Model II (p. 87)
See Appendix for abridged version
Chapter 7: Learning Model II Behavior
Part III: Practice . . . all interesting but note
    especially Chapter 10: Redesigning Professional
    Education

theories of practice

governing variables	action strategies	consequences for behavioral world	consequences for learning

model I

1. Define goals and try to achieve them.	• Design & Manage the environment	• Actor seen as: defensive inconsistent competitive selfish	• Self-sealing
2. Maximize winning and minimize losing	• Own and control the task	• Defensive interpersonal & group relationship	• Single-loop learning
3. Minimize generating or expressing negative feelings	• Unilaterally protect yourself	• Low freedom of choice, internal commitment & risk-taking	• Little testing of theories publicly; much testing privately
4. Be rational	• Unilaterally protect others from being hurt	• Defensive norms like mistrust, lack of risk-taking, emphasis on diplomacy	

model II

1. Valid information	• Design situations or environments where participants can be originators and can experience personal causation	• Actor minimally defensive, seen as: facilitator collaborator choice creator	• Freedom of choice & authenticity
2. Free and informed choice	• Tasks controlled jointly	• Minimally defensive	• Double loop learning
3. Internal commitment to choice	• Protection of self is a joint enterprise & oriented to growth • Bilateral protection of others	• Learning oriented norms: trust individuality, open confrontation	• Public testing of theories

Argyris & Schon: p. 21,68,87

ii. design knowledge

Three kinds of knowledge: (outlined by Posner):

1. PRECEDURAL memory refers to "how-to" action and related behavior consisting of rote, motor (walking and drawing) and conscious, cognitive behavior (design, layout, document development).

2. SYMBOLIC memory refers to "whats" that are totally abstracted from the real world.

3. ICONIC memory refers to objects and concepts that are triggered externally e.g., the knowledge of physical objects.

Iconic Schemata: Posner suggests a generalized knowledge representation called schemata which are formed through our ability to abstract universal qualities of individual objects and produce a general description. One of the primary memories in design is iconic -- recognizing, recalling and manipulating physical objects. We have the ability to organize schemata hierarchically for complex objects. Each schema must be versatile enough to allow us to recognize all sorts of different examples of a similar object . . . e.g., different types of roof lines.

Symbolic Schemata: Reasoning is our ability to infer new information from existing -- informal methods of reasoning dominate design behavior. Unlike logical inference making, informal reasoning is inexact. The rules are often intuitive and the causal sources derive from personal knowledge. Formal system of inference use IF-THEN structures such as if A, then B where A and B are any symbol, sets of symbols or descriptors -- e.g., if hot, then open window. The IF-THEN process allows us to state implications from premises.

Procedure Schemata: These schemata deal with the knowledge of what to do, when to do it, and how, during design. An experienced designer has a catalogue of "strategies" as to how to deal with "inferences." The strategies are examples of conflict resolution, a heuristic device (a rule of thumb which tends to reduce the number of issues to be considered or operations applied to reaching a goal). Trial and error is another common heuristic device.

SUGGESTED READINGS: **The Science of the Artificial** by H. Simon

Cognition: An Introduction by M. I. Posner

Teaching Architecture by Omer Akin (ASCA 1981)

iii. development of design theories

Verification/Cycle Research: This idea contends that a cycle such as the design/build/monitor cycle could be a key to the development of design theory. "Theory" needs to be built in explicitly at the start of a cycle experiment. "You design the theory into the building (or landscape) in order to test it; and in monitoring, you know, as a result, what you are initially looking for" (Maxwell, 1970, p. 466). The results of cycle research should inform design teaching; cycle research itself in the studio is impossible because students do not **build** buildings which can be occupied or tested. He suggests that we need testing mechanism (computers?) -- that opinions are not sufficient instruments. Stringer (1975, p. 635) argues for devising design problems in the studio which make **verifiable** solutions possible and that the frustrating aspect is that students rarely produce anything which can be tested.

Integration: Design depends on knowledge found in many fields of study. Many design disciplines are guilty of "theory borrowing" in the name of interdisciplinary research. Instead theories should be sought which integrate fields. Climate modification concepts and environmental history are examples of potential sources of integrative theory. Integrative ability does not emerge somehow magically, merely by the process of designing something. Hillier and Musgrove both argue that the typical analysis to synthesis model of the design process does not result in integrative behavior and instead is an unreal description of designing -- one that has been derived from a wrong interpretation of science. Instead they suggest a model based around elements that are essential definitions of buildings or spaces e.g., symbolic or cultural objects.

Nature of Synthesis: There is a belief in the importance of developing a theory of synthesis in design. Simon (1969) made a case for the recognition of design as a central activity in all professions. Schon (1974, pp. 3, 20) argues that

> attempts to reduce the design process to a sequence of decisions programmed in a decision structure turn out to assume as 'given' what most needs explanation -- the basic design 'structure.'

 BEST REFERENCE: **Architecture Education Study** Paper: "Analysis of the Content of Design" by Julian Beinart

SUGGESTED READINGS: **The Sciences of the Artificial** by H. Simon

Hillier, Musgrove and O'Sullivan: "Knowledge and Design." EDRA, 1972

Maxwell: "Teaching and Learning." RIBA Journal
Volume 77 Number 10, October 1970, pp.
463-466;

Stringer: "The Myths of Architectural Creativity."
Architectural Design, October 1975, pp. 63-65

ARCHITECTURE EDUCATION STUDY
Consortium of East Coast Schools of Architecture
Volume I: The Papers, Volume II: The Cases

This two volume compilation, funded by the Andrew Mellon Foundation in 1974, began from an expressed concern for the lack of fit between architecture education and the demands of changing society and practice. It focused on the study of learning in design studios. Observations, in the form of cases, are at the core of the **Architecture Education Study (AES)**. Much of the learning research was directed by Julian Beinart, a professor at MIT School of Architecture and Planning. He was assisted by Chris Argyris and Donald Schon (**Theories in Practice**), authorities on organizational behavior and on education process. The Beinart group selected three case studies to be conducted in schools of diverse location and nature. Two of these cases are reported in detail in Volume II. Volume I contains seven papers, four of which are described in Recommended Reading.

Recommended Reading:

The AES was the singular most pertinent source that was found for design education. It illuminated many situations in the design studio that related to the processes of teaching and learning. The following four papers are recommended reading as is Volume II: The Cases.

Analysis of the Content of Design: Julian Beinart

Beinart describes the AES case data in relation to what is taught and learned in the studio. He reports that the major concepts that describe the case studies are determined by choices made by teachers and students in the studio setting. These concepts are tempered by forces like perspectives held on outside architectural practice and the goals of the students.

Structure of the Content of Design: Julian Beinart

This second paper reflects on the structure of knowledge in studio education against the backdrop of history and recent writings in architectural education. He describes three models of relationships among teachers, students and knowledge systems. See chart on following page.

Learning a Language, Learning to Design: Donald Schon

Schon links case information to theories of instruction and interpersonal behavior to show what is intended to be taught and learned. He observes the connection between verbal (talking) and non-verbal (drawing) components of the "language" of designers. How students respond to this new language determines the students' studio experience. He concludes that: ". . . designing competence is the ability to reflect in action and to hold ideas loosely."

Teaching and Learning in Design Settings: Chris Argyris

Argyris studied the interactive behavior in the design studio as revealed through verbal exchanges. Based on the theories from **Theory in Practice** he claims there is a gap between espoused theories and theories-in-use. He found inconsistencies in the case material between what the instructors stated were their objectives and what actually transpired in the studio. Problem solving became increasingly ineffective when process and criteria were not discernible. As a result, according to Argyris, "instructors encouraged student dependence; over time, mystery came to be taken as a symptom of mastery." Instructors could reduce student dependence by making the processes more explicit.

students, teachers and knowledge

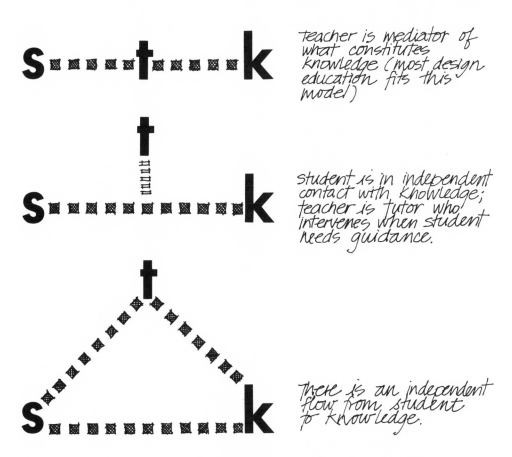

teacher is mediator of what constitutes knowledge (most design education fits this model)

student is in independent contact with knowledge; teacher is tutor who intervenes when student needs guidance.

there is an independent flow from student to knowledge.

Architecture Education Study: p. 221

summary

Short Cuts, along with the Annotated Bibliography, is a report on the literature review conducted as part of the **Ideabook.** The preceeding pages are brief summaries of key ideas and theories in the field of philosophy, psychology and education. The literature review concentrated on finding sources that related to the theoretical aspects of teaching, revealing a wealth of information from the three broad fields contrasted by a dearth of information on design education.

Short Cuts also serves as background and context for the IDEAS THAT WORK in the following chapter.

3. IDEAS THAT WORK

IDEAS THAT WORK

This chapter is the core of **The Ideabook.** Approximately 250 ideas, including those from interviews and literature survey, were evaluated and edited. The format for this chapter is designed for the busy person. A keyword system is used to group common ideas and allow indexing and potential computer access. Primary keywords are located at the bottom right hand corner of each page, accompanied by a visual symbol. The second hierarchy of keywords or phrases is located at the page top just above the ideas. The page is divided into three zones. The first is graphic only. For readers flipping through **The Ideabook** these graphic images show the gist of the ideas. The more diligent reader goes on to the IDEA itself which is displayed prominently center page in point form. Within the IDEA, tertiary keywords are printed in uppercase. Finally, the truly committed proceed to the third zone for expansion of the idea. These usually include quotes from various design instructors interviewed. Associated with the comments are the source of the idea, if from printed material, and any reference to another related area.

Chapter Organization:

ORGANIZING AND PREPARING
    state your biases
    teaching approaches
    educational and instructional objectives
    course outline
    appropriate teaching methods
    keep options open
    physical space

SHOWING AND TELLING
    the stage is set
    the performance
    hardware

RESPONDING
    students helping students
    teachers helping teachers
    students responding to teachers
    teachers responding to students
    general response

PROJECTS
    general
    specific

ORGANIZING PREPARING

ORGANIZATION is important in teaching. The goal is a creation of an orderly, functional and yet exciting experience. People like order -- at least to some degree. If they are learning something new which might be foreign or frustrating, the existence of some framework of order is welcome and essential as a reference point, a feeling of accomplishment and well-being. This framework is the responsibility of the teacher.

Organizing and preparing for teaching design may be defined by the following steps:

1. state your biases

2. choose a teaching approach

3. write educational and instructional objectives

4. write the course outline

5. think about appropriate teaching methods

6. keep options open

7. be conscious of physical space

The first person to organize is yourself. A datebook to ensure appointments, deadlines, etc., are met is necessary for most people. The absent-minded professor routine is not humorous, especially to students whose time and money are as valuable as your own. The organization of a course involves general decisions on objectives, subject matter, scheduling and responsibilities. If you are organized and your course is organized, students will easily organize themselves -- and they will by the role model set by you.

It was difficult to elicit specific ideas on organizing from the interviews -- too often statements were truisms without concrete examples to make a specific point. More valuable information about writing course objectives came from the literature review. When asked about physical studio space, few interviewees had experience with other than traditional studio spaces to draw on for practical suggestions. There was concern about specific desk layouts within studios but rarely did instructors hope to move to a different mode or physical space in the near future. The ideas were, instead, presented in the form of wishful thinking. Teachers are busy enough from day to day; there is rarely enough energy to instigate totally new environments or processes that have potential to rock the "administrative" boat.

PREPARATION develops from organization. If organization involves decision-making for subject matter, scheduling and responsibilities at a general level, then **preparation** is the filling in of the blanks with specific "goods" for day-to-day instruction. Proper preparation is time and energy consuming, but without it even a well-organized course is like a hollow box. Students respect the teacher who is well organized in general and well prepared for the day's specific activities.

How much preparation is really required? Good instruction is the professional obligation of the instructor -- how long does it take to prepare a professional presentation? Personal standards and experience, and potential to build on previous work will determine the required commitment. There is always temptation to cut corners on preparation due to time constraints. Fight it. Preparation is essential and obligatory.

Good concrete ideas came out of questions on preparation -- especially about course outlines that connect specific with general educational objectives. Preparation was mentioned as important by most instructors. There was little information on exactly how much time preparation took except from one instructor in architectural history who allows ten hours of preparation time per lecture -- this is after he has presented the course for the fifth time and already written the lecture. More specifics are needed, from experienced teachers, on time allotment. Source books are needed to make preparation more efficient as materials tend to be spread far and wide. Subject outlines, with annotated bibliographies, would help beginning teachers prepare sessions on grading, design vocabulary or behavioral annotations. Otherwise, every teacher does his/her own; taking time away from students.

state your biases

Be aware of your belief and value systems and the ideologies they support. An educational ideology is a reference point for the teaching part of our lives. Confusion is minimized when teachers are explicit about their biases and values.

IDEA: State your BIASES clearly at the outset of a studio . . .

> What I say is my opinion or viewpoint. Students should entertain it and a general openness to other viewpoints. I want it to be clear that there is no right or wrong -- only levels of appropriateness.

IDEA: Do a problem with the students to expose your BIASES and PROCESS . . .

> When I teach a design studio I occasionally do the problem with the students and also present it. Both learn a lot this way - - they see the way I operate and they better understand my biases and the basis of my design philosophies.

IDEA: Establish a PHILOSOPHICAL BASIS in a broad sense for all work in the studio . . .

> It is important when beginning a studio to have some discussion of the philosophical basis of what we are doing. What is unique to the approach we are taking? Where does it fit into the general framework of thinking on the subject?

IDEA: Structure projects in such a way that biases and values are CENTRAL ISSUES to the design solution . . .

> Allow students to be explicit about their own values at the outset of a project, then evaluate with them at the end whether or not their designs reflected those espoused values. More often than not, they **don't!**

ORGANIZING

approaches

The following is an accounting of some existing studio approaches. These models are developed from a study by Michael Jordan of Auburn University[8] and hybridized for the purposes of the **Ideabook.** See Chapter 4 for further elaboration.

THE THEORETICAL MODELS are based on theories -- social/behavioral and visual (abstract and graphics). The chart on page 51 compares THE ABSTRACT OBJECT STUDIO, THE DRAWING STUDIO and THE AWARENESS DEVELOPMENT STUDIO.

THE PRAGMATIC MODELS are concerned with issues relating directly to building or space design (after the fashion of the Beaux Arts). The chart on page 52 compares THE REAL DESIGN STUDIO, METHODOLOGY DEVELOPMENT STUDIO and THE TECHNOLOGY STUDIO.

THE ADVOCACY MODELS are based on the desire of students and young professionals to become competent and useful in helping disadvantaged people and resolving social problems. The chart on page 53 compares THE SOCIAL AND ECONOMIC PROGRAMMING STUDIO, THE COMMUNITY ACTION STUDIO, and THE HOLISTIC ECOLOGICAL STUDIO.

THEORETICAL MODELS

	ABSTRACT OBJECT	DRAWING	AWARENESS DEVELOPMENT
instructional emphasis	.work with theories about the abstract notion of design .derive principles to be eventually applied to real situations	.drawing, graphic skills and communication of ideas .emphasize plans, sections and drafting skills	.increase sensitivity of student to self and context .based in behavioral/social science techniques
approach	.designer as artist or craftsperson-recognizing few constraints	.designer as worker or artist .look, see, copy and thus learn	.designer as culturally and socially conscious
comments	.projects manipulate specified and limited materials in an inventive way to solve basic physical and aesthetic problems	.limited intellectual base .ignore social and self awareness .produces "production" designers	.little emphasis on traditional design .often loosely structured and dependent on faculty for direction .thorough bibliography ."sensitive" studio matter
teacher/student relationship	.teacher as studio master and critic	.teacher as critic	
ideology	.intellectualism: (abstract ideas and theory)	.conservatism: (emphasis on basic skills)	.liberationism: (emphasis on self-understanding)

PRAGMATIC MODELS

	'REAL DESIGN'	METHODOLOGY	TECHNOLOGY
instructional emphasis	.simulated or real design problems from the outset .basic design fundamentals learned through exposure and critique .aesthetic values and realism important	.developing problem solving methodolgy aimed at a defensible conclusion based on data .applicable to any problem	.mathematically derived optimal solutions .usually structural or engineered
approach	.designer as worker (corporate)	.designer as armchair analyst, philosophize and theorize	.designer as engineer/builder .physical determinism
comments	.no text or bibliography .intellectual base is a product of problem consideration and teacher's design approach	.projects involve reading, writing, computers .structured process-oriented approach	.projects involve investigation of materials and structures .advanced technical awareness
teacher/student relationship	.teacher as master and and critic	.teacher as co-thinker/ researcher	.teacher as master and critic
ideology	.intellectualism	.intellectualism	.intellectualism

ADVOCACY MODELS

	SOCIO-ECONOMIC PROGRAMMING	COMMUNITY ACTION	HOLISTIC ECOLOGICAL
instructional emphasis	.focused on social and economic design issues .programming from a user viewpoint but within the system	.learn design with a framework of reality; integral with community .facilitation and understanding of interpersonal and environmental process	.emphasis on "knowing why" .design as an experiment of various methods concerned with people and place
approach	.designer as programmer and policy maker	.designer as facilitator, value informed	.designer as specialist design/builder *from Koh
comments	.limited exposure to traditional skills .emphasis on creative to real issues	.limited exposure to traditional skills .need to find new employment niches	.value-full with emphasis on ecological/evolutionary ethics .learn theories but apply experimentally
teacher/student relationship	.teacher as co-worker	.teacher as coordinator	.teacher as resource person
ideology	.liberationism	.liberationism	.liberationism

educational and instructional **objectives**

IDEA: Use a DESIGN SEQUENCE FRAMEWORK to develop a course with educational objectives in mind . . .

One department has established Core Goals such as . . .

1. Develop a land ethic and aesthetic philosophy
2. Develop a problem solving and design ability
3. Develop technical ability

They have also evolved Support Goals such as . . .

1. Develop self-awareness
2. Develop communication abilities
3. Develop cultural awareness

These goals are then connected to the four years of the program and ways to achieve these goals are considered through approach, project type, field trips and readings. This system makes objectives very explicit as well as providing a comprehensive course outline. It combines both.

On the following pages are an example of a draft design sequence framework from Cal Poly Pomona, Department of Landscape Architecture.

design sequence framework

EDUCATIONAL OBJECTIVES

CORE GOALS	1st LEVEL FIRST YEAR	2nd LEVEL SECOND YEAR	3rd LEVEL THIRD YEAR	4th LEVEL FOURTH YEAR	5th LEVEL
Develop a Land Ethic and Aesthetic Philosophy	Environmental awareness Sensory aware-ness .visual .tactile .acoustical .olfactorial Land stewart-ship	Landscape apprecia-tion .Space .Form .Color .Texture Landscape character Visual Resource management	Ecological under-standing human ecology natural ecology Locational variables Materials and energy flows	Issue Understanding parties to the problem economic deter-minants political process	Professionalism .consultant .advocate .decision maker .administrator
Develop Problem Solving and Design Ability	Creative thinking .graphic idea-tion .sketching .brainstorming Basic design principles .composistion .proportion .color .scale .structure	Problem awareness and solving approaches .problem definition .problem solution Form determinants .human .natural (Using Design Problem Method)	Design Methods process .research .analysis .synthesis .evaluation Form making .physical design Context .urban .social deter-minants .rural	Planning Methods process .research .analysis .sythesis .evaluation Policy making .physical planning Context .urban .rural	Professionalism role: .consultant .advocate .decision maker .administrator (Case Study Method)

design sequence framework

EDUCATIONAL OBJECTIVES

CORE GOALS	1st LEVEL FIRST YEAR	2nd LEVEL SECOND YEAR	3rd LEVEL THIRD YEAR	4th LEVEL FOURTH YEAR	5th LEVEL
Develop Problem Solving and Design Ability (con't)	Study models photography		.natural determinants		
	(Using Diary or Journal)		(Using Design Project Method)	(Using Planning Project Method)	
Develop Technical Ability	Human factors .scale .comfort zones .sensory .perception	Natural factors .solar orientation .micro climate .plants .soils .hydrology	Man-made circ. systems .vehicular systems .pedestrian systems .utility systems Natural systems .energy flow .water flow .sediment flow .nutrient flow	Construction systems .land form .planting .structures .drainage .plumbing .electrical	Political and economic systems .communication .political process .decision making process .business practice .cash flow

56

IDEA: A course description tells of the content and procedure . . . a COURSE OBJECTIVE describes the desired outcome . . . what the learner is supposed to be like as a result of the process . . .

A meaningfully stated objective is one that succeeds in communicating to the reader, the writer's instructional intent. The course objective should communicate what the learner will be able to DO or to PERFORM at the end of the course.

IDEA: Repeat course objectives frequently . . .

Make course objectives as explicit and purposeful as possible. It is important to make them clear and to repeat them in various forms -- verbal, written and graphic (see example on page 58).

IDEA: Limit the content of sessions through CLEAR and PRECISELY stated expectations . . .

Each class session, each project, each drawing, each evaluation and each visit should be preceded by the proposal and group acceptance of written and then verbalized educational objectives.

PREPARING

sample course objective

The Situation: The general objective of this studio project is to demonstrate design for accountability -- the necessity for, and the utility of, user-based information in design. The project is an iterative design process involving two or more consecutive solutions for the same problem and context. One design/evaluation cycle will be done using only traditional building/space programs e.g., sizes and requirements. Succeeding cycles will use the same traditional program with additional appropriate behavioral and user-based information supplements.

REMEMBER the five components of an instructional objective:

1. WHO is to perform the activity?

2. The observable ACTIVITY to be performed.

3. The PRODUCT, performance or result of the activity.

4. The relevant CONDITIONS under which the activity is to be performed.

5. The standard or criterion used to EVALUATE the activity.

Sample Instructional Objective for this specific project

Given a traditional building/space program and a user-based information supplement, STUDENTS will produce, in a two week studio session, several design alternatives. Using the same problem and context, they will first apply only the traditional program and then add the user-based supplement. Students will produce ANNOTATED AXONOMETRIC DRAWINGS on trace which will indicate exactly where and how solutions demonstrate accountability to program supplement materials. EVALUATION will be based on the degree of accountability: the evaluator may choose any item from the supplementary material at random and then observe where it manifests itself in the design.

This project was derived from "Teaching Design for Mainstreaming the Handicapped" by Cohen and Hunter, pp. 54-55.

PREPARING

project and course outlines

IDEA: Prepare COURSE OUTLINE so there is a definite structure to the studio session . . .

I never feel welded to my course outline if there is good reason to change, but it is important for it to be well-articulated and simply -- CLEAR. In this way students can set unknowns and organizational frustration aside, and get on with the project (see example on page 59).

IDEA: Let students know WHAT IS EXPECTED and WHAT TO EXPECT . . .

It is vital to allow students the courtesy and the security of knowing clearly the expectations around the studio. This leaves their minds and "worry boxes" clear for design issues.

IDEA: Use a COURSE OUTLINE MATRIX as a technique to choreograph the class . . .

The main matrix headings are General Topic, In Class, Problem Assigned and Due, Demonstration, Field Trip, Guest Speaker, Reading, Teaching Devices and Other. These go along the top of the page and are lined up against the dates of the different studio sessions. The teacher can then fill in the blanks of what is happening each session. This gives a sense of rhythm for the class and xerox reductions can be handed out as typical class schedules (see example on page 61).

IDEA: Your project statements or any handout material should set a good example of clear WRITING and interesting GRAPHIC layout . . .

I look upon each course outline or project statement as a design project in itself -- in this way it is fun to create and is a good example for students to follow (see example on page 62).

PREPARING

sample course outline

DESCRIPTION

COURSE: Design Education Seminar (6 units)
TITLE: Introduction to Teaching Design
OFFERED: Rarely, a chance of a lifetime
CLASS MEETINGS: Two 1 hour discussions per week and two 3
   hour practice teaching sessions per week
PREREQUISITES: Philosophy of Education, Education Psychology
INSTRUCTORS: Various faculty
FINAL EXAMINATION: None
STUDENT HOURS PER WEEK: 8 hours in class, 10 outside class
EVALUATION: 50 percent on journal; 50 percent on participation
ATTENDANCE: Required for all class meetings

OBJECTIVES

Design Education 100 is an introductory seminar in teaching design. The participants are 3 faculty members and 10 students. Students will gain theoretical and practical exposure to teaching design. They will research and compile design theories from literature and experience. These theories will then be discussed in the seminar and students will write instructional objectives and outlines to teach the various areas of theory. Practical experience will be gained by instituting instructional objectives and outline in an afternoon session with a group of students. The remainder of the seminar class will observe the student teacher in action and later evaluate the performance of the teacher and effectiveness of the instructional objectives and outline to teach a particular theory. Students will keep a journal of their experiences and will be evaluated on journal completion and participation.

STUDENT ASSIGNMENTS

1. Major course projects: literature review and research into a specified area of design theory; formulation of these theories into coherent segments; description of course objective and outlines to teach each segment; institution outline and evaluation teaching technique.

2. Assigned weekly readings will supplement the projects.

3. Annotated sketchbook/journals will record the process.

PREPARING

60

sample course framework

LARC 100 fall 1984

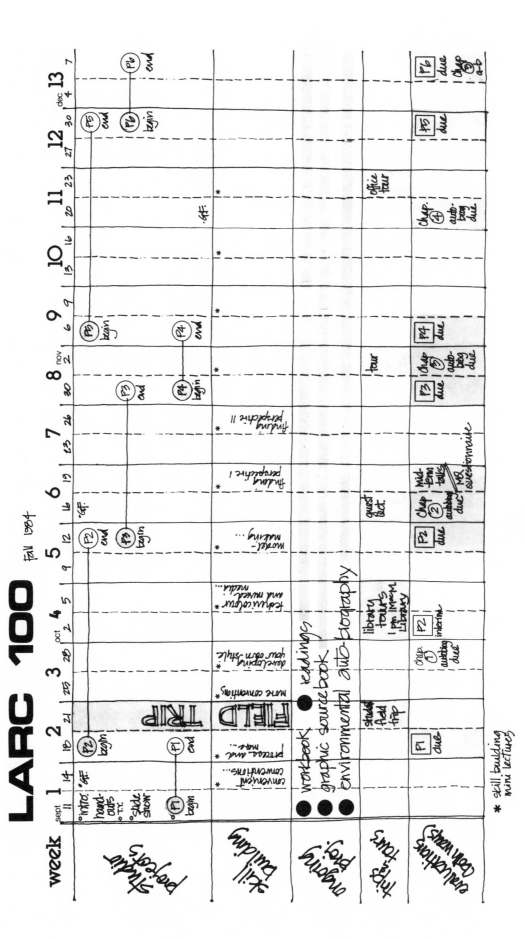

LARC 100
Project 4
Fall 1984

intervention

An intervention occurs so as to modify an action or expectation.

"How sad would be November if we had no knowledge of the spring!"
      EDWIN WAY TEALE, 1953.

"November's sky is chill and drear
 November's leaf is read and sear"
      SIR WALTER SCOTT, Marmion, 1808.

a celebratory intervention

November is a month in need of celebration. Create and implement a
landscape intervention in a public space that celebrates November.
In other words design and construct a celebratory modification to a
specific site realizing the constraints of time, money & legality.

Document the ideation and design process including site information
in your sketchbooks; record the completed intervention in situ with
colour slides. Materials: anything you can find or buy within
reason.

Presentation format: a choreographed slide show by the class
presenting the interventions on Friday November 16, 1:30 p.m.

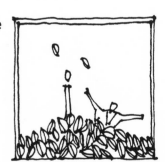

Objectives: to offer a break from the theoretical processes of the
            past weeks thus emphasizing the opportunity to
            actually alter the landscape, albeit suddenly for a
            short duration, and enjoy the creative process.

            to explore the notion of "intervention" in an
            environmental sense.

            to gain experience preparing slide shows as
            communication devices.

Evaluation: 1. RISK TAKING (demonstrated willingness to take
            risks, to try out new and different ideas)
            2. CONCEPT-IDEA (project has a strong functional-image
            concept; having form, commodity and delight)
            3. CONTEXT (work in context with problem to be solved)
            4. ENVIROMENTAL & PEOPLE SENSITIVE
            5. IMAGE CLARITY (clear image development in terms of
            symbolism, materials, shapes, forms, colours,
            metaphors and similes)

teaching methods

IDEA: A quick (10 minute) slide lecture or black board explanation with a handout and problem to solve is useful for COMMUNICATING FACTUAL INFORMATION . . .

I like to have handouts ready to add to students' personal information manuals every class session. It further emphasizes the point-- to hear, see and read.

IDEA: Technical information is distributed to students in the form of INFORMATION PACKAGES which provide the foundation for their own PERSONAL REFERENCE MANUALS . . .

These manuals are developed by students to serve their own personal requirements and information needs. A workbook could easily be developed for learning factual material (for instance in a site planning studio) with readings, mini-problems, etc. These could be coordinated with larger studio problems, but would be done by the students at their own pace.

IDEA: Reinforce lectures before and after with READINGS, EXAMPLES and DOING . . .

It is important to suggest readings prior to a lecture, to lecture with good examples and then go on a field trip or have a problem in which they DO whatever is involved in the problem (see example on page 64).

PREPARING

sample teaching process for factual material

Define instructional objective: Students will be taught the concept of SITE ANALYSIS through readings, lectures and finally by doing an analysis. This study will occur in a two week period and will be evaluated on the basis of thoroughness of the project site analysis (criteria to be included in future hand-out) in covering the factors discussed and the success at giving priority to important information.

PRIOR TO LECTURE: (5 days) assign readings emphasizing the variety of approaches to looking at sites: e.g., **Design with Nature** (McHarg), **Mysteries and Realities of the Site** (Richard Neutra), **Site and Enviromental Planning** (Rubenstein) as well as pertinent journal articles.

LECTURE: (1) Discuss philosophies of sites as related to readings. (2) Use a sample case study to consider the factors: natural, cultural, people, visual. Show examples of these factors in side-by-side slides -- one showing real photography and the other a clear graphic representation of consideration for the specific factor.

HAND-OUT WITH LECTURE: Distribute and discuss handout with site analysis factor checklist.

PROJECT: Distribute project statement clearly stating the site location, how to use the site analysis checklist, and the requirement of one trace overlay for each general factor grouping, documenting the necessary information.

PIN UP (day project is due): Students can pin up overlays and an informal discussion can result from comparisons and questions.

DEBRIEFING: (a few days after the project): Discuss process, product and future use of the skill learned.

IDEA: Hold an independent SEMINAR in parallel with a design studio . . . hopefully with two different groups of students . . .

Students in such a seminar undertakes several projects:

1. They monitor problem solving processes of one of the students in the studio over the entire term;

2. They assist in identification and form development of user criteria;

3. They explore various aspects of user criteria in terms of character, use and influence on design.

The objectives of this seminar, according to the author, are the opportunity for both seminar and studio groups to focus more directly on the processes of design, to enrich the programatic materials and processes available to the studio and to assess the relations and uses of criteria in design.

IDEA: Hold a night SEMINAR to complement the studio . . . with the same group of students . . .

This provides a change of pace and gives the studio work more breadth. If done in conjunction with other studio classes it gives exposure to many different professors and students and new attitudes.

IDEA: In the ENGINEERING APPROACH students are supplied with most of the technical information and skills needed by theoretical courses before they are exposed to a design problem . . .

We give them basics, theory and applications. Often their design experience derive solely from the apprenticeship in an office.

IDEA: Studios could be supplemented by skill-building SHORT COURSES or WORKSHOPS that supply intense experience and information in a short time . . .

These short spurts provide a needed sense of accomplishment in the midst of a longer project in the design studio. They are useful to expose students to other teachers or experts in certain fields. These workshops could vary in orientation from specific graphic techniques, to group process techniques or an identifiable skill that could be handled in a short session.

IDEA: The OMNIBUS model of studio organization allows many courses to be integrated into one large project . . .

For example, in architecture, two weeks might be spent on color relationships, dealt with by a specific faculty member who introduces general concepts, some small problems and advances the work on the larger problem. Separate issues are then always in context of the major project. It seems there might be an advantage too for the faculty to have two week stints in various studios -- more variety and challenge.

IDEA: FIELD TRIPS are an essential part of studio structure and broaden the students' horizons . . .

The important thing on a field trip is to raise questions . . . Why does it work? Why do you like this place? It is difficult but important for students to analyze good composition or good design or to feel sense of scale and the size of spaces.

Getting people into the field is the answer! We all learn so much by experiencing in a group the kinds of things we only talk about or view from slides in the normal studio setting.

the field trip

keep options open

IDEA: Work required by the course should be feasible in the amount of TIME given . . . there should be relatively little work required during out-of-studio hours . . .

> What would happen if the studio doors were locked between 10 p.m. and 6 a.m.? The only work to go on would be reading or sketching or thinking . . . not production on the drawing board. We might begin to evolve more efficient and sensible designers.

IDEA: Design a studio with PACE and RHYTHM in mind . . .

> I carefully study the calendar of the studio session I will teach. Using what I call "Line Energy Choreography" I take holidays into account so I know when I can get full attention. I make a conscious decision on how I would like the energy to go . . . when to peak, when to slide, when to blitz and how to take them out high.

IDEA: SCHEDULING IS IMPORTANT . . .

> It is imperative to have a series of closely spaced deadlines so that students can arrive at and evaluate the design. The process should be speeded up in the beginning with care taken to ensure projects are scaled appropriately with enough intellectual meat. Every class day should be scheduled -- usually with something due and often with a sketch problem in the first hour.

IDEA: Structure an 8 a.m. EVENT for a class that runs from 8 a.m. to 12 noon to which people from the profession come and talk and "sit on the hot seat" . . .

> This kind of event allows students to drift in as they will but makes sure that there is a structured beginning to the class. Eventually students realize they are missing something if they do not arrive at 8 for the event. The studio must have a structured place to do this kind of a coffee hour to start off the day.

IDEA: A LUNCH-BAG LECTURE series can be a good way of introducing new ideas and methods into all the studio courses of a program . . .

This kind of series can involve students with special expertise or experiences as well as professors or people from outside the university. The lectures can be about travel, different approaches to being designers -- any theme that relates remotely to design. It seems like a good format for ideas and opinions are different from the typical studio.

IDEA: Learning is a BUILDING PROCESS so it is important to start off with a project or event to which students can personally relate . . .

Learning is a challenge and we derive fun and satisfaction from improving ourselves. To begin his classes in plant materials one instructor assigns an essay on what things have given the students an interest in plants or any biases. It is important to reveal biases at this time so we connect our past to our present and the students connect our past to our present and the students can say -- ah-ha that's why I like deciduous trees or wood detailing. It is also vital to start with some known quantities and build new information on that base.

lunch bag lecture

physical space

IDEA: The studio should be set up with many VISUAL IMAGES to stimulate people and start them thinking and drawing . . .

Implications of images, ideas and attitudes are important and the environment of the studio should be full of visuals. It should be collectively geared to stimulate the senses as well as being a social space.

IDEA: Create a newer, EXCITING space . . .

The spaces are too monotonous in most of our schools. We need more variety. Try out a store-front city studio, a remote wilderness cabin or whatever else you can imagine. Students will have ideas but its your job to facilitate them.

IDEA: Institute the UNIVERSITY ARCHITECTURAL DIG SYSTEM . . .

This idea centers around the use of remote and mobile study facilities in the scope of national participation. This alternative responds to lower projected student enrollments, lower budgets and the need for more direct involvement with environmental systems. We need to establish an "inter-university" system that allows and encourages sharing of students, faculty, equipment, study and research opportunities. Establish, in common, an array of uniquely located and equipped work/live/play "base camps" throughout the nation, utilizing mobile life-support vehicles. Sometimes the best educational setting is not the campus; it is where what you want to study is happening. (Brian Kesner, ACSA, 1981)

SHOWING TELLING

Visual or experiential images are inherent in design, however it is important to realize the need for appropriate, carefully selected images to maximize the educational process. A variety of techniques are available to assist in SHOWING, from the old page-burning opaque projectors to current computerized graphic displays. The well prepared design teacher has endless visual resources to use as examples. It is the matter of exposure to visuals and ideas that becomes the role of the teacher, especially for undergraduates. If they have not traveled or grown up in certain specific environments then they have not been exposed to enough ideas or images to allow them to draw easily on their experiences. It is the teacher's job to help them explore new territory.

Specific, usable ideas came from questions on **showing**. The ideas of "instant" slides from a polaroid slide camera and the "on site shows" are appealing. Communicating visually is a forte of most design teachers -- they are stimulated by visuals themselves and see the importance of communicating these skills to their students. Design teachers communicate most clearly when they draw; they no doubt do not draw enough in front of students.

Show and **Tell** combine for powerful communication. Verbal communication has the potential to demand attention and stimulate the imagination, but it is not easy. Speaking well is an art, described by such qualities as rhythm, projection, organization, modulation and distinction. Delivery should be audible and interesting. Too much wisdom is lost through boring presentation.

Teachers must speak clearly to communicate ideas. The combination of good delivery and substantial knowledge is, unfortunately, all too rare. Professional jargon does not help.

Most of the ideas on **"telling"** came from the literature. Teachers, especially those who depend on the lecture format, must be good "tellers." Design teachers depend so heavily on visuals that telling skills are rarely exercised. The instructors interviewed rarely referred to "talking" in terms of differences between addressing a large group or an individual. Useful ideas came from Sondra Napell's **T. A. Training Handbook**, especially the section on non-facilitating teaching behaviors. The notion of sufficient wait time calls on the teacher to be patient after a concept has been aired; it gives the students time to respond and participate. This method has been found to be very effective in group juries where, given enough time to respond, students contribute significantly.

the stage is set

IDEA: WHAT IS THE POINT . . .

It is too easy to throw many images together in the form of a slide show and expect them to talk for you. Instead it is important to find simple and dramatic slides that make your point.

You must use words to explain the slides that are consistent with the pictures. Remember that images dominate what we hear. The image will always win -- but it is still important to support the image with chosen words.

Often two contrasting slides shown side by side offer more stimulus to discussion and focus material more than a 30 minute slide show.

IDEA: ROLE PLAYING requires direction . . .

I found that students got a lot out of role playing exercises when a facilitator, like myself, was present to generate some information and energy. Without a facilitator -- they seemed ineffective. After the role-playing, we discovered there were many reactions and different insights about what they felt in regard to the site and the program as well as surfacing of some deeply held feelings.

IDEA: Actors (students) create a story about some profession and idea (suggestions from audience) in two minutes and all the dialogue must be in the form of questions . . .

Watching and taking part in such improvisation is stimulating, for it is similar, if not quite so demanding, as the design process. It frees people up to think quickly, improvise and improves verbal skills.

IDEA: Take typical role-playing one step farther to theatre and DRESS for the occasion . . .

In a history of world gardens course the students dress for each garden type -- e.g., Persian gardens or Japanese gardens. This way they begin to understand what happened socially in the garden, more of its symbolic meaning and why gardens were designed in different ways.

IDEA: SIMULATE projects using people and available studio materials as props . . .

In one project students simulated the university campus which they were studying. Various students became buildings, a blue ribbon was the water course and presto -- the theatre began. In a sense it was a living history of the campus . . . as the years chimed away from the campanile (a very tall person on a pedestal), buildings were built and demolished. Those not representing buildings or landscape were on the stage watching the evolution of the campus in 3D form as the years passed. It was a good way to teach process.

IDEA: Encourage students to ROLE PLAY in informal crits . . .

If students play roles other than themselves in informal project discussions, it exposes them to totally new viewpoints and allows a safe crossing of the lines. They can comment on the work of their fellow students in the capacity of the role without feeling they are dishing out personal criticism. It also helps them see their project in a different light.

IDEA: Use PEOPLE FORMATIONS to show scale and distance on site . . .

Given a large, open site (about 5-25 acres) use students to help get a sense of scale by having them line the perimeter of the site, make grid formations at 50 foot intervals and by splitting into groups and sending off specific numbers to show how that many people are perceived on the open site. It is a graphic way to get students to relate to scale.

IDEA: Make site visits at night, in the rain, at all different times . . .

IDEA: Be a PACK RAT . . . do not throw old notes away . . . at least make sure they are stored in a computer . . .

Too often I have made the mistake of thinking I will never do that lecture again and no sooner have I discarded my notes but need them urgently.

the performance ...preparing and delivering

IDEA: The success of a lecture is PREPARATION . . . preparing for lectures is different from preparing to answer questions as one might as a student . . .

An excellent down to earth source for help in lecturing is Donald Bligh's book called: **What is the Use of Lectures?** (See Bibliography)

IDEA: Suggestions for a good lecture . . .

1. Establish favorable rapport by chatting or exchanging words with students.

2. Put lecture outline on the board or use some visual material.

3. Begin with a few questions relating to the last topic and tying in to the present discussion.

4. Present topic in well organized blocks of 15 minutes maximum.

5. Be sensitive to audience reaction symptoms such as posture and rustling.

6. Conclude in time to allow questions, discussion and review.

7. Prepare and adhere to lecture outline and course assignments so students can engage in preparation before and after.

8. Couple lectures with small group study.

I like to start a lecture calmly with my recap, then I tend to get carried away and involved with what I am saying and discover that time is running out . . . then I have to speed up . . . I want it to be fresh for me and for them -- and that is hard work.

Varying pace is one way to keep a lecture interesting. If I am showing slides, I try to slow down -- otherwise I keep up the pace. Having your own "sense of theatre" is helpful for bringing "electricity" into your presentation.

TELLING

IDEA: Allow your PERSONALITY to come out when you are telling . . .

I do not like video, it is not in REAL TIME, it is too complex and it kills the LIVE nature of life. It takes too much time of what I like to call "kitchen work" or busy work getting it together. Instead I feel we need a different sense of theatre in our work -- it has to have soul and personality as main ingredients.

IDEA: Get COMMUNICATION going and initiate questions by posing questions . . .

I have to remember not to get enthralled with my own ability to talk. It is better for students to discover things for themselves. If there are no questions after I lecture I am suspicious -- either no one has understood, they are all asleep or I have explained it so well there is nothing else to ask. I try to ask questions that bring up other questions and that frequently gets things going.

IDEA: Use INDUCTIVE QUESTIONS (they cannot be answered by a simple yes or no or factual answer) to instigate mental action . . .

Inductive questions necessitate mental investment and energy. They fall into some categories: Clarity Questions (**Could you expand upon that thought?**); Awareness Questions (**Why is that true?**); Relational Questions (**How does "X" relate to this idea?**); Prediction Questions (**What can you predict to be the consequences of this activity?**), and Focus Questions (**Do you agree with that premise? Restate what you understand.**) (Walt Cudnohofsky)

We need to reinstate daily, especially for younger students, the habit of using our minds. In addition, there is no better way than for teachers to model the skill of producing good inductive questions.

The next three ideas from Sondra Hapell's **TA Training Handbook** suggest ways to change common non-facilitating teacher behaviors . . .

At issue is the relationship between intent and actions: What teachers do and how they do it delivers more impact than what they say. (Sondra Napell, **TA Training Handbook** p. 2.1).

IDEA: Allow SUFFICIENT WAIT TIME . . .

Wait time is the interval after an initial question has been posed -- before a teacher answers it her/himself, repeats, rephrases or adds new information. More than a few seconds are necessary for mental information processing to provide enough time for quiet thinking. Try to increase wait time from one second to at least three to five seconds. Think deliberately about expanding the time and share this concept with students.

Wait time is important especially in juries where student comments are sometimes difficult to solicit. If the teacher can manage to keep quiet long enough -- the students contribute in a manner that is useful and interesting. This allows the teacher to act as a resource person and summarizer.

IDEA: Beware of RAPID REWARD . . .

What happens when instructors say to the first respondent to a question: "Right, good." As if to assure that further thinking will stop, the teacher proceeds to reword, repeat or move on. People learn at different rates. Encourage student-to-student dialogues by extending the silence after an answer is proffered, giving questioning glances to other students, ask "what is the analysis of what was just said?" or changing your physical proximity in the room.

IDEA: Keep your own EGO under control . . .

Students need to feel psychologically "safe" to participate, to try out ideas, and to be wrong as well as right. Avoid phrases such as "Since I have explained this several times already you all should know . . ." and "obviously . . ." Remember and refer to student ideas, frame open-ended questions and acknowledge your own fallibility.

hardware

IDEA: Have easy access to a POLAROID SLIDE CAMERA to make instant slides . . .

I have a polaroid slide camera set up on a tripod, always ready for action. It produces instant slides of my quick sketches or ones out of books -- all ready for my next lecture.

IDEA: Use a 3-minute VIDEO (like a commercial) to explain specific processes . . .

This is the TV generation so this kind of tool makes sense in a lecture setting -- it adds variety and makes an impression. On the exam 95 percent of the class got the question right that had been explained by the mini-video.

IDEA: Use VIDEO for teaching site analysis techniques and for communicating various issues to students or public . . .

Video tapes, whose target audience is beginning design students, can explore basic design principles in 30 minutes. There is further potential to video sites as a survey tool or to give students exposure to good design works.

IDEA: Use SUPER 8 film for showing . . .

Super 8 film is not as soft and mushy as video; it is more expensive and it forces me to be more focussed. I also like the time lapse capability of the Super 8. I do use video as a research tool but it seems not as useful for teaching -- except for recording student presentations.

IDEA: Develop COMPUTER LITERACY for . . .

1. Number crunching in computer based calculations like cut and fill or structural calculations . . .

2. Computer-based drafting . . .

3. Three-dimensional perspectives (interactive graphics for designing) . . .

SHOWING

4. Two-dimensional mapping (computerized McHarg) . . .

5. Word processing . . .

I see using the three-dimensional interactive graphics in design studios for designing. I could also see generating solar access information for certain housing developments that students might be working on.

IDEA: Take PHOTOS of student work . . .

I take slides of all student work to use later on in the same session to make points or show progress and also to use in other courses. They are a wonderful resource but are not helpful unless catalogued immediately in a way that gives easy access.

IDEA: VIDEODISCS . . . a new technology visual recording medium . . .

Videodiscs promise ease of use, cost effectiveness, durability and greater interface with computerized projection facilities. They are presently under research and development. (New Directions for Teaching and Learning series: **Technologies** edited by C. K. Knapper)

IDEA: VIDEOTEX . . . long-distance transmitting of visual information . . .

Videotex is a means of transmitting visual information over long distances using either broadcast or telephone means. It requires a small decoder attachment for the television and can be tailored to specific user needs. Videotex is presently under research and development.

RESPONDING

RESPONDING involves seeing and listening, the implicit ability to understand, and the ability to communicate new ideas. Understanding may involve knowledge or compassion, or both, and is the key to responding in effective dialogue with others. Teachers must regularly ask themselves whether they are giving students sufficient opportunity to question or comment, and whether teachers have sufficient communication among themselves. Again preparation is the key to overcoming defensive or insensitive responses. The necessary politics and psychology in establishing good rapport are always a challenge.

The responding ideas were the most interesting and stimulating. The instructors were all interested in different ways of responding to students and each other. More specific ideas are needed about teachers helping teachers. Time to communicate and support each other is easily squeezed out by daily demands. No revolutionary ideas were suggested on how to improve the whole field of response through crits or juries, although each instructor expressed concern about the most effective ways to criticize.

students helping students

IDEA: Create LEARNING CO-OPS of three to four students that come together to help each other . . .

The individuals in the co-ops are responsible for one aspect of the mutual skill development of all the people in the group. Generally, people are placed because of their strengths and weaknesses. This allows students with special skills to share them and increases interaction among students. The faculty are not members; they act as resource participants by suggesting guided readings or specific activities.

IDEA: Students EXCHANGE PROJECTS for an hour or so and work on a colleague's problem . . .

I like this system of stirring things up in the studio -- if students get too immersed in their own issues they lose perspective on what they are doing.

IDEA: Each student prepares a set of working drawings and supplies prints to another student who CRITIQUES the drawings . . .

I add more comments to each check set and return them to the author. This method really tests knowledge of more technical nature -- I use this for construction classes where there are more or less right and wrong answers.

IDEA: Students helping themselves through Personalized System of Instruction (P.S.I.) . . .

Students learn through reading, lectures, demonstrations and field trips. There are weekly quizzes which are used as diagnostic rather than punitive methods. There is immediate feedback on the quizzes and students can write them again at any time. Problems are dealt with on a one-to-one basis and each student has a chart of his or her progress so procrastination is kept to a minimum. This system has been used in more lecture oriented classes such as horticulture where factual information is weighty, although the philosophy of this system could be applied to studio courses to give students more responsibility to go at their own pace.

RESPONDING

IDEA: A room to house all the LEARNING SYSTEMS such as P.S.I., slides tapes, videos and computers with user-friendly instructions is a valuable addition to a studio . . .

IDEA: Assign a lower division student to an upper division one for advising, help and support . . .

IDEA: BUZZ GROUPS can address specific issues and break up lectures . . .

Four or five people turn in their seats and do one of the following: clarify confusing parts of a reading assignment or lecture; list questions everyone in the buzz group would like answered; choose topics everyone in the buzz group would like to have pursued in a lecture or discuss a problem and report on it in 10 minutes.

buzz groups

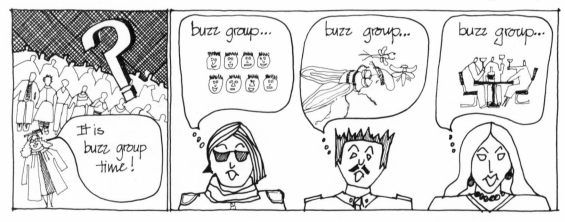

RESPONDING

teachers helping teachers

IDEA: OBSERVE other teachers in action . . .

> Teachers should make a point of watching other teachers in action. If someone on your campus won an outstanding teaching award -- go to their lecture/studio and evaluate what and how they do it.

IDEA: Use campus facilities to have yourself VIDEO-TAPED during a lecture or to help you design a mid-course EVALUATION . . .

> There are numerous education resource people on campuses to help teachers. They hold teaching workshops and have up-to-date information on teaching methods.

IDEA: Institute a FACULTY RETREAT to keep communication lines open among the faculty . . .

> The faculty retreat seems like a good way to get in touch with what other faculty are doing and thinking. It benefits the students from the point of view of increasing continuity as they proceed within the program. At the retreat we discuss the profession, design studios, curriculum, morale -- we generally use it as an opportunity to air feelings in a place and space apart from the university.

IDEA: Write up HOW and WHAT you are teaching at the end of each course . . .

> Writing up a studio experience should be part of the evaluation process. It makes sense that the more teachers report on their experiments and exploration, the more other teachers and students can benefit. By "making permanent" the experience, it seems to open up your professional life to a welcome scrutiny from your peers and thus opens up more regular communication among faculty.

IDEA: In large groups communication of AGENDAS and IDEAS is crucial . . .

When teaching large groups (100 students) there is usually a team of teachers. It is important to understand what is at stake for each of the team members and that it takes many repeated courses with the team to fine tune the system. Regular staff meetings are necessary to keep up communication -- include written minutes each week to report on decisions.

IDEA: The pros of TEAM TEACHING . . .

Team Teaching is useful because two or more teachers can "call" each other on things they believe or do not believe. It gives the students some permission to disagree. It is also the perfect opportunity to show there is no right or wrong with design. Colleagues from other disciplines bring a wealth of knowledge from their specific fields that make the extra organizational effort worthwhile.

IDEA: The cons of TEAM TEACHING . . .

Teaching is a personal thing and it is difficult to organize with another teacher for the best results.

team teaching

RESPONDING

students responding to teachers

IDEA: Set up a mid-session CONFERENCE with each student to discuss his or her progress . . .

Student evaluations at the end of a session are a problem. They are useless to people in that particular class. I try to hold personal talks so I can get some notion of how I am doing as a teacher. It is important to get feedback on my work -- I try to talk to students about this at desk crits as well. The conference sessions have the advantage of being more individual and private.

IDEA: Look for tell-tale CLUES for how well you are doing . . . attendance, how many people are staying late out of interest to talk about the project . . .

I try to keep eye contact, especially with key people, to keep me in line. I get a sense from their facial expression whether I am losing them or they are bored or extremely interested. I attempt to alter course in a lecture or discussion depending on the senses I get from eye contact.

IDEA: DEBRIEF a day or two after a project has been completed . . .

A debriefing is a chance to discuss the strengths and weaknesses of the project, the process and how the class felt about the experience. It is an opportunity to talk which can be followed by a chance for students to write additional comments to me. It is an important feedback mechanism.

IDEA: Become familiar with students and their backgrounds by handing out QUESTIONNAIRES . . .

Knowing with whom I am working with, in the sense of who my students are and what they already know, helps me to direct the course to the best level and gives me an idea of the interests and motivations in the class (see example on page 84).

RESPONDING

sample 'beginning' questionnaire

The following is a sample questionnaire, in this case for a class in planting design . . .

GETTING TO KNOW YOU

To better know each of you, please take a minute to answer these questions:

1. Name

2. Previous plant-related courses you have taken, including botany, etc.

3. Design studios taken in the department?

4. Estimated number of plants you know well (#   ) or with which you are somewhat familiar (#   )?

5. Briefly state your prior experience outside school related to gardening, horticulture, planting design, etc.

6. What are you special interests in the field of design?

7. What objectives do you hope to achieve by taking this course?

8. Which of the following places have you visited on field trips? (list common "sites")

(Questionnaire from Russ Beatty, UC Berkeley, Department of Landscape Architecture)

RESPONDING

The following are alternative ideas to typical university end-of-course questionnaires. These ideas come from a handout by Teaching Innovation and Evaluation Services (TIES) at University of California at Berkeley. The end of course questionnaire can provide some relevant information but comes back to the instructor at a time when it is already too late to make any changes which might benefit the students doing the evaluation. The information is also too general to give instructors specific guidance.

IDEA: Borrow student class notes . . .

> Periodically borrow students' notes to see whether the main ideas are getting across and to identify problems students may be having with the material. Of course you need to alert students that you will be doing this during the term so that they do not feel as if their privacy has been invaded.

IDEA: Assign MINUTE PAPERS . . .

> Assign "minute papers" at the end of some of your classes. These papers consist of two questions on which students are asked to write for a minute or two at the end of a particular class session. The questions are: (1) What is the most significant thing you learned today? (2) What question is uppermost in your mind at the end of today's session? These papers can be useful sources of information in evaluating their thoughts and writing their ideas.

> The idea of minute papers could be used in design studios to focus on particular design concepts or to help summarize certain studio events.

IDEA: VIDEOTAPE the class . . .

> While it can be a startling experience, videotaping is an effective way of finding out whether an instructor dominates a discussion, the nature of questions asked, whether sufficient time is allowed to let students think through questions, and other factors related to discussion techniques. This would also be helpful in studio crit and discussion sessions for evaluation of teacher and student "performances."

RESPONDING

SAMPLE END OF SESSION QUESTIONNAIRE (evaluates the course more than the teacher)

The following are sample questions from various end of session questionnaires:

sample 'ending' questionnaire

What specific areas of knowledge do you think you have gained from this course?

What areas would you like to learn more about, develop further, if there were succeeding courses? (For example, a studio which applied some of the ideas or principles to a design problem).

What three specific pieces of information from the course do you feel to be the most valuable to you and why?

How much of the readings did you actually do? _____ %.

Did you attend the discussion sections? Were they helpful? How could they be improved?

Please make suggestions for improvements and changes to the assignments (in the case of the social factors in design class the projects were specifically the behavioral analysis of plaza users, a post-occupancy evaluation of an open space and an environmental autobiography).

Do you have comments on the overall content and organization of the course?

The single most positive aspect of the course was:

The single most negative aspect of the course was:

Do you have suggestions of how this course could be better connected to other courses in the curriculum, or how the "message" of the course can be carried through to design studios?

(These questions come from Clare Cooper Marcus: LA 140 Social and Behavioral Factors in Design, U.C. Berkeley and from Marc Treib and Ron Herman: ED 178 Japanese Architecture and its Environment, U.C. Berkeley.)

RESPONDING

teachers responding to students

IDEA: Use DESK CRITS for imparting factual information . . .

When a specific problem arises, make use of it at an individual desk crit to deal with some factual material in context. This method can be used with a group of students but experience indicates that the student whose specific work it is benefits the most.

IDEA: Take 10 minutes alone with the student's work and ANNOTATE feelings and criticism directly on plans and sketches . . .

This way students do not just have a verbal crit but after I have left they have my comments to read and consider. It also gives me an opportunity to really think about the projects, concentrate and be concise and useful. I like the system.

IDEA: Run PROGRESS PRINTS to mark up and return to students . . .

Make sure there is a print machine in the studio. At the end of some class sessions I have the students run prints of "where they are," I collect them, comment on them and return them as soon as possible. It forces me to keep up and gives the students fairly immediate written feedback.

IDEA: Bring together three to four students to talk as a group about their projects . . .

This group "tack-up" is less intimidating and is a non-linear approach to generating discussion. I feel desk crits are too time wasteful and inefficient. In most studios we just cannot afford it.

IDEA: In group crits enforce the rule that EVERYONE MUST COMMENT about the design in question . . .

The reason is that the work belongs to all of us and I want to develop critical thinking and articulate speaking in my students. If they have to articulate their values and explain themselves -- it is good practice.

RESPONDING

IDEA: Talk about what the student has DONE not what they have omitted or forgotten . . .

I think of feedback as intentional criticism in that I direct my comments to what the student has done. In this way the student can remain with you on the rocky ride of the discussion. Criticism, after all, is worth something -- it is investment and ideas. Teachers should avoid saying "you should not" or "you must not." Ultimatums do nothing to encourage or build on what the student is doing.

IDEA: Hand pick your jury for interesting and verbal people . . . for POSITIVE REINFORCERS, not cynics . . .

It is the responsibility of the professor in charge to give you continuity and criticism in the context of the problem during jury crits. It is also important to have guests. Someone other than yourself can introduce different value systems and argue different points of view.

IDEA: Old fashioned JURIES have advantages . . .

I like the old-fashioned jury. It is important that students know what we think about what they have done and other students learn from hearing criticism of different works. I do not like to invite outside people who are rarely fully aware of the problem.

IDEA: Have the jury look at the work in advance . . . they prepare a PRESENTATION to the students . . .

The jury looks at the projects and interprets the drawings . . . the students then can take notes on the commentary as part of a project journal and ask questions of the jury.

IDEA: SMALL GROUP presentations . . . four to five students, one jury member and one faculty member . . .

This method allows time for every student to present and for some personal feedback both from peers and from jurors. I believe that videotaping each presentation is valuable as a record for the presenter to review and to allow better feedback on presentation techniques.

IDEA: Bring people from RELATED DISCIPLINES for juries . . .

It is difficult to bring in a lot of people from the outside. I like to have one or two people from related fields -- like sociologists, psychologists, artists or clients. Other designers tend to confuse rather than clarify issues.

IDEA: Use COMPREHENSIVE GRADING SHEETS to explain grading procedures . . .

I got tired of hearing . . . "Why didn't I get an A?" I hand out grading sheets with certain categories of what I was looking for. I have five grades from poor to excellent to which I assign points for each category. At the end I can add them up and give a total. This grading sheet and the criteria for grading should be discussed at the beginning of the project (see example on the following page)

IDEA: Use the SPECTRUM POLICY in reviewing design projects . . .

The spectrum policy gives you both sides of a problem. By definition you get an understanding of another person's idea or situation because you really lend your mind to it; you temporarily keep quiet about your concerns. Next you talk about what you like in the new idea. This lets the person know that your intent is not to put down his/her ideas. Finally you express your concerns. In reviewing site plans this policy can be used by having a reviewer address two issues: (1) What do I like about the project? and (2) What would I like to see more of? (From Alon Kvashny: "Enhancing Creativity in Landscape Architecture Education." **Landscape Journal**, Vol. 1, No. 2, p. 109.)

RESPONDING

sample grading sheet

Project Evaluation **DESIGN**

Primary Criteria: Sensitivity to site conditions;
                  social patterns, and
                  neighborhood environments

Necessary Elements:

Integrates with community - visual   - /4
                           - accessibility
Buffers adjacent land use - sight and sound - /4

Respects and enhances creek zone   - /4
Preserves 70-90% of existing vegetation   - /4
Incorporates existing vegetation into   - /4
    proposed vegetative massing

Provides required dwelling units (20-24)   - /2.5
Provides required parking spaces (30-36)   - /2.5
Provides required recreational spaces   - /2.5
Provides vehicular (including services)   - /2.5
    access and pedestrian access

Site organization provides a variety of   - /4
    spaces and site environments
Circulation system clearly organized,   - /4
    with minimum conflicts: pedestrian
    priority
Solution respects children, teens, working
    adults, seniors and physically   - /4
Day/night and seasonal use of site accom-   - /4
    modated
Structures oriented for positive solar   - /4
    access and views
                                            _____
                                             /50

Project Evaluation **COMMUNICATION**

      REQUIRED SUBMISSIONS

          Model   - /50
          Sections (2)   - /10
          Sketch (1)   - /10
          Concept Diagram   - /10
          Design Process Diagram   - / 5
          Objectives and User Biog. - / 5

                                    _____
                                     /50

Comments: _____

general response

IDEA: Help students see what their own PROCESS is . . .   they should become self-conscious about how they solve problems . . .

The ideal situation is when the teacher works with the student enough to begin to understand the student's process and discuss it with him/her. In team work, encourage students to observe the way other people solve problems and report on different ways to each other.

Students should record their process as part of studio time and activity.

IDEA: There are always ALTERNATIVES . . .

I can often see fear in students, especially about decision making or putting pencil to paper. In preliminary phase I encourage them to produce as many alternatives as possible, always on trace with no presentations -- just some one-to-one crits. The final drawing should evolve later. This way also allows time for students to be conscious of their process.

IDEA: Encourage students to take 15 minutes and STAND ON THEIR HEAD to think about the problem . . . the key is to encourage students to think in different modes . . .

The notion of synectics or making the strange familiar and the familiar strange is good to introduce into design studios. For instance, when you do a site analysis pretend you are the site . . . what does it feel and say? The good problem solver is able to switch gears between the different modes.

IDEA: Assign small PROBLEMS to be accomplished in a short space of time (10-20 minutes), post them and have a discussion to launch into a subject . . .

IDEA: Take people on GROUP RETREATS . . .

The idea is to take a break from the routine of the system and to go away. It is the perfect opportunity to participate together as a group, to get to know one another and to get mileage out of discussions that in a different setting would go nowhere.

RESPONDING

IDEA: Emphasize in the students' design processes that PEOPLE and the BUILT ENVIRONMENT are out there for us to study . . . an open and available laboratory . . .

Only too often there is an underlying message in a studio class that prior solutions to the same design are of no consequence. A similar concept is that innovations and new solutions are the absolute goal and are deemed to be the BEST in terms of aesthetic breakthroughs. By setting a small post-occupancy evaluation problem at the start of the studio, students learn to look with a questioning eye. I make the explicit suggestion that existing examples are worthy of study and full of design-related information.

IDEA: Teachers should be considered as RESOURCE PEOPLE . . .

The instructor should be considered a resource person, not a studio critic. The idea of apprentice and master should be dropped in favor of the tutorial, workshop or study method approach.

RESPONDING

# PROJECTS

Choosing projects is an important part of teaching design. Projects should be orchestrated for incremental learning and the educational objectives of a project should be clear. Writing the project statement clearly, providing enough base information and including criteria for evaluation are all important components to beginning studios. If time-consuming research is not an objective, care should be taken to ensure that sufficient information is presented in the problem statement so that the students might concentrate on the relevant objectives. In advanced studios, some flexibility is desired in projects -- to the point where a "choose your own" process is the most acceptable.

Projects vary according to the type of teaching approach in a studio. For instance, traditionally the one hundred trees in the field problem would find no place in the community action studio; it is considered too abstract and theoretical. In the same sense, a studio oriented to explaining basic visual principles would not use a complex socially-oriented project. However, it is the mixing of these concepts that make a project and studio richer and more valuable.

Some good ideas came out of the interviews. Instructors answered the project questions with ease and enjoyment. Projects are the tangible "goods" of the design experience which are easy to talk about and describe. Projects are also appealing because often they are the products of an instructor's own design process and creative response.

The following section describes some approaches to projects in general and then lists some specific projects to give design teachers new ideas or inspiration.

general

IDEA: Assign two design problems simultaneously, each with a distinctly different emphasis . . .

> This stops students from being trapped into deadend solutions by forcing them to work on the second project a while, therefore giving the students an opportunity to look at the first project with a different view.

IDEA: Set the DUE DATE for a major project two weeks before the end of the term . . . give a series of sketch problems related to the project in that time . . .

> Often the problem in design process is prolonging the decisions -- resulting in the student's inability to explore further his or her solution. Once the decision is forced upon them by the due date, a much more relaxed atmosphere can prevail in which they can investigate several aspects of their solutions in a quick sketch form.

IDEA: Occasionally take the ANALYTICAL APPROACH towards designing a project . . .

> One such project is to dissect the ordinances of a standard subdivision and of a planned unit development -- and compare the two.

IDEA: Use a series of exercises in beginning landscape design studios that breaks down the landscape components and likens them to ELEMENTS of a ROOM . . .

> The students look at the FLOOR (paving, ground plane), WALLS (trees, earthforms) and CEILINGS (tree canopies, etc.) in light of concepts like entrance, sequence, role of sunlight and effect on space, visual interest and human comfort.

PROJECTS

IDEA: More studio projects should involve REDESIGN . . .

After all, in the future we are not going to be always building the new -- we will be renovating the old. Re-design problems are challenging ones that make the student look at the whole world of existing information readily and visually available from which they can learn.

IDEA: Students need to know how to USE the environment and its elements that they see . . . they need to know how to translate them to an applicable form for use in design . . .

We should be teaching students how to extract the grammar and composition of a sentence in the sense of looking at a space and taking it apart. What we can do in introductory design studios is teach a new vocabulary or language -- a visual language.

IDEA: Ask the students to apply a series of ADJECTIVES to the space they are beginning to design as part of the process . . . when the design exercise is complete it is possible to evaluate how successful they were at creating a space that could be described by the adjectives . . .

At the beginning of a design exercise I give the students a list of adjectives and their opposites (the semantic differential list from Osgoode's book: **The Measurement of Meaning**) like empty/full, angular/rounded, ferocious/peaceful, rough/smooth or pungent/bland. It is a method to start to understand the feelings of spaces. It is important that the adjectives are not necessarily architectural ones.

IDEA: The longer project emphasizes PROCESS . . .

I like starting with a small sketch problem, but after that I like to have the students get intensely involved in one project -- so they can get the most out of it.

I look at the results of a longer problem and then focus on weaknesses that I see with shorter problems. For instance before students do a housing project, they are assigned a quick that might be designing a little building.

PROJECTS

IDEA: SHORTER projects break up the term with a variety of things to do . . . LONGER projects tend to make students delay making decisions . . .

I like to use problems that are of a highly specific nature that are shorter to support a longer project. The short project might teach things like edges, connections, vocabulary broadening while the long project might teach site planning process.

IDEA: A studio built around a COMMUNITY PROJECT exposes students to a variety of problems and lets them get a feel for a community . . .

I am often approached by communities with a project, so working with the community group becomes the studio structure to the extent that the agency will often donate space to allow the studio to happen in the community. I see myself as the connector between the class and the community group.

IDEA: The COMMUNITY PROJECT that runs for a longer period of time is the most satisfying studio from the learning and teaching viewpoint . . .

Motivation for work comes for the students, not from the teacher, but from taking on the problem and wanting to work on the solutions. This is in fact the "practice" model of studio that is modified by realities of the education system.

specific

IDEA: A PERSONAL OBSERVATION WALK . . . learning to look with new eyes and for a variety of reasons . . . critically looking at various aspects of our lives . . .

Incorporated into the script for the sensory walk are exercises in awareness of movement, pattern, form, light, texture and also experiments in mass observation and interaction both with buildings and people. The purpose is to make people aware of how their own perceptual processes influence their assumptions and expectations about the environment.

PROJECTS

IDEA: Encourage students to keep a JOURNAL of the experiences in the studio . . .

Students learn a lot from collecting information and observations in a journal or notebook as the studio progresses. This keeps them looking at the environment and gets them prepared for the idea of always having a sketchbook for ideas--their own or other peoples'.

I insist that journal keeping not be included in the work of the studio but that it becomes another class with attached units and resulting responsibility.

IDEA: Use basic PROBLEM SOLVING projects that are simple to state but interesting to solve . . .

One project is designing a device so you could drop an egg to the pavement from four stories so it won't break. Another is the design of a water feature that will produce musical tones.

IDEA: Ask students to make daily entries in a personal journal or diary which reflect their observations in the year 2050 . . .

Future planners and designers need to have an understanding of the possible impact of current and future actions on person-person and person-space relations. Give them hints like the following for starting their journals . . . you are an important settlement planner, you are a counter-culture radical, you are a rigid and conforming mainstream person, you are a narrowly specialized scientist, you are the BIG BOSS of the whole cosmos . . . (from Ralph Goebel, University of Wisconsin S-P).

IDEA: Send students on an imaginary tour for three to four minutes and then have them quickly put down their thoughts graphically in drawings or clay forms . . . commonly called GUIDED FANTASIES . . .

We talk seriously about what they produce and why. It is powerful to produce something so quickly and to realize that it is not trivial but often quite vital and perceptive.

PROJECTS

IDEA: Students evaluate and re-design a PRODUCT . . .

Students are assigned a project to choose an object in a hardware or grocery store that they feel is poorly designed. They must analyze the function and design a new device or prototype to do the same job. A sequel to this project is to design the advertising packaging for the project.

IDEA: CARDBOARD CITY . . . a formal exercise in space and full size construction . . .

In the rear courtyard of Wurster Hall a fixed ground plan is established. The site plan is designed on a three feet by three feet grid with spaces having urban analogs implied. Each student draws his/her site by lottery. The problem statement asks each student to design a defined space for seating which includes various constraints. Marc Treib writes in his **JAE** article Vol. 35, No. 3: "The cardboard city problem was invented as a formal exercise in space and full-size construction. It became evident quite soon, however, that it was as much a political structuring project as it was one of form. There is no type of design without political decision."

IDEA: Design a PARADE as a spirit generator . . . the whole parade including floats, events, the route, the type of music . . . all are part of the project . . . as in PARTICIPATING . . .

The one year we did this problem, we had 5000 students on campus joining the parade. It gives spirit and impetus to get on with other design problems. It is a real energy generator.

IDEA: Add 100 trees to an open field . . .

This is a two day "abstract" problem to make students aware of sun/shade, climate, etc., and spaces created by trees. The site is a flat field (no dealing with topo) on which students can place a maximum of 100 trees of any one species -- on one acre of the site. The space is used for walking through. The problem is simple, yet sophisticated. Some students find it a challenge, others find it too abstract.

PROJECTS

IDEA: Create a PLACE for a marriage (or any other kinds of ceremony) . . .

In this problem, students invent everything -- clients, users, site, topography, vegetation, etc. They find out about creating a place and what is necessary to "accommodate" the ceremony. Issues such as natural vs. man-made in place-making become important.

IDEA: Replace a CONVENTIONAL CONTEXT with a startling one . . .

An example would be an interior perspective, altered through the addition of an unexpected element. One project is entitled "The Disaster" and asks the student to draw his room as if there had been a natural disaster. This requires that each student go through the steps of creating a "straight" drawing, and that he or she then experiment with ways to extent the initial drawing in depicting a situation which does not actually exist. (Tony Dubovsky, **Drawing in Context**)

IDEA: Create a FULL SCALE design experience . . .

The project was to create shelters for two people -- to design, fabricate, transport and reassemble them on site. After they were erected, the students were required to live in the environments and pay the price for what they had created. It was necessary for the students to deal with all the practical problems of any developers -- zoning, setbacks, etc. (Source: Donald Heil)

IDEA: Use a CONSTRUCTIVE PROCESS that is real to set the studio tone
. . .

On the first class meeting, I walked in and announced that the class would be hosting a sit-down dinner for 60 (for themselves and one invited guest). I lay $100 on the table and left for coffee. When I returned, they were catatonic. But as soon as I started to break the problem down into bite size chunks, they started to get into it. They established group and specific tasks and in four days time sixty people were sitting down, at one table, to a multi-course meal, complete with entertainment. And you ask . . . is this design? And I say of course . . . the whole thing was about the problem solving process. And above all, it built trust and confidence among the students. It set a tone of cooperation and really knocked out individual competitiveness. It set the mood for a good studio.

PROJECTS

IDEA: Set up projects to look at and EVALUATE built works . . .

One idea is to send students in groups of two's out to investigate issues or projects, such as different housing projects, take pictures and come back and report to the group on what they have seen -- in the form of sketches or slides and accompanying commentary.

IDEA: Take classes away from the formal studio and let them EXPERIMENT with materials . . .

I like to take my design studio classes to the beach to experiment with sand casts and plaster of paris. The students work in pairs and begin to understand shape and form as well as organization and confusion. It is a participatory kind of problem that works well to get a class going.

IDEA: Design an ISLAND as an oasis with a certain program . . . then evaluate it . . .

Evaluation can be in terms of . . . How many people could the island hold comfortably? How many could the island hold densely packed? How many experiences can people have on the island? List them. How many pauses? How many different things can they reach out and touch?

IDEA: Introduce CONSULTANTS and OBSERVERS into the studio . . . like the elderly, the disabled or kids depending on the project . . .

The way in which we teach students about others greatly affects how they understand what we have taught and how they will eventually apply it while working professionally for others. In my view, there is no substitute for face-to-face contact in acquiring this kind of knowledge: physical disability and architectural access are meaningless unless taught within a context of human experience. (Ray Lifchez in **JAE**, Vol. 31, No. 3)

Incorporating different people into the studio experience as consultants to the students on their design problems is one way to create this context. The most difficult thing is to explain to students that these people are consultants with a certain expertise and are not their clients whom they must "please."

IDEA: Give students RESPONSIBILITY in defining the direction of their work . . .

Replace the traditional studio program -- designing a building type -- with a social issue which becomes the theme for the course. After a period of discussion and a photographic essay as field work on the issue, the student then outlines, in a unique statement of intent, reflecting his/her personal interest in the social issue, a proposal for an environmental solution which addresses the social issue. Therefore the student is given responsibility to define direction. (Ray Lifchez: "From Inside to Outside -- a Journey to Architecture" in **JAE**, Vol. 27, No. 1)

IDEA: Use SCENARIOS to help students design . . .

A useful technique for assisting students realize important human issues is story-telling or scenarios. By telling a convincing story about how a design works in human terms the student can clearly see how his/her design responds to human needs. Scenarios are essentially a way of speculating on how people will use a place to focus how the design should be made.

IDEA: The concept of SUPPORT, FILL and ACTION . . .

It is helpful for students to have recognizable categories or parts of a design. One concept, from Ray Lifchez, is that of support, fill and action. SUPPORT, in architecture is the building which is immutable. FILL is the furniture or those things that people bring with them to a space. ACTION is of two types -- observable and hidden. Observable action is what people do that we can see -- eating, drinking, playing. Hidden action is feelings and thoughts. Using these categories it is clearer to see the decision that designers must make and the influences we have over support, fill and action. How much support is necessary and how much is the people's own "fill?" This means one must think carefully about all three.

IDEA: Students write biographies of the users or they themselves as a group become the "using clients" . . .

This allows intimate knowledge and contact with users. Students can use scale photos of characters to put in their design models to add reality to the characters they have created.

PROJECTS

IDEA: Students follow a process to produce their own VALUES STATEMENT
. . .

Students are asked to read a treatise or polemic writing by a conventionally accepted hero e.g., Frank Lloyd Wright. They must ferret out a values statement as might be written by the "hero." The next step is for students to reflect on their own past work, their character and personality. Out of this reflection comes their own personal values statement. This assignment is often fraught with pain and turmoil as people, whether they are 20 or 50 years of age, have difficulty committing themselves to specific values or ideologies.

IDEA: To expose VALUES students are asked to map, draw or write about their favorite childhood places . . . could be extended to be an ENVIRONMENTAL AUTOBIOGRAPHY . . .

This exercise gives everyone a common beginning point. It is important the first day to put expectations out on the table -- those of the professors and the students. Thinking back, a lot of my expectations come from my own studio experience and I have to be aware of that.

It is important to learn about our own design values and biases -- it is a necessary parallel form of learning to look more deeply at yourself and your biases. The point of writing an autobiography about personal experiences with environments is to increase awareness of ourselves and of others.

IDEA: Allow students to choose a project and a ROLE to take in undertaking the project . . .

For instance, one team might take the typical design or planning consultant role as if consulting to a city. Another team might choose an entrepreneurial role as developers looking at design, market, financing in which a "proforma" is the end product. Another student might take the advocate role on an issue like the preservation of hills around a campus in which the product is a series of newspaper columns and community meeting reports. This exposure to a range of roles makes the projects lively and interesting for all. It is also a way to encourage a broadening of the scope of designer in the traditional sense.

summary

Ideas That Work is a compilation of many ideas about teaching design. It is a start to exploring the resources -- especially the many design instructors across North America.

Big Ideas, the next chapter, builds on the information from **Short Cuts** and **Ideas That Work** to identify main issues and directions for future work.

4. BIG IDEAS

BIG IDEAS...

This chapter is a personal commentary on the **Ideabook**. The first section, BIG IDEAS, is a synthesis of the literature review and interviews. The second, WHAT NEXT?, is a comment on the **Ideabook** and an outline plan for further research and expansion.

 A. BIG IDEAS

Short Cuts and **Ideas That Work** are based on different research methods. BIG IDEAS presents issues as a format for discussing the information from the previous chapters. The issues are:

where to start...
design knowledge...
perspectives...
design education models...
teaching roles and styles...
mystery and mastery...

where to start... design with a big 'D'

Formal design education begins relatively late in the span of years considered "prime" for learning. There is much literature to support the contention that the three R's (reading, writing and arithmetic) have dominated the school system with such power that visual development is effectively blocked at an early age. Therefore, people rarely have an opportunity to explore their visual potential. Psychologist I. MacFarland Smith writes

> Our current system of education actively discriminates against the student who is competent in spatial ability.[9]

Why has design education (thinking visually, problem solving, etc.) been so ignored by the North American school system? The British experience points to some of the reasons.

Design education is becoming a recognized and established subject in the school system in Britain. But, according to Anita Cross of the Open University at Milton Keynes, two issues limit its development.[10] The first is the emphasis within the subject on specific career preparation and the second is the lack of genuine educational framework for the subject. According to Cross, design theories need to be organized in the same manner as general education theories and principles. The basic skills and ways of knowing design surely have a place beside literacy and numeracy as fundamental aspects of education. Bruce Archer conceptualizes this relationship as follows:[11]

areas of human knowledge   Archer: p. 20

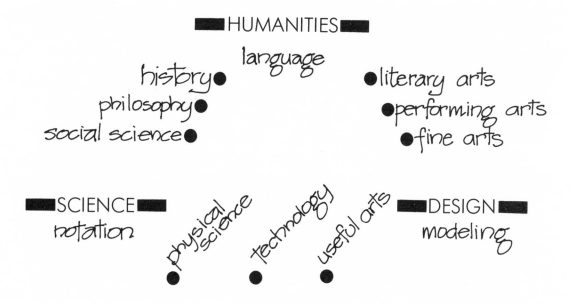

107

While SCIENCE is the collected body of theoretical knowledge based on observation, measurement and hypotheses, and the HUMANITIES is the collected body of interpretive knowledge based on contemplation, criticism, evaluation and discourse, the third area is the collected body of practical knowledge based upon sensibility, invention, validation and implementation.[12] Design with a big "D" has been used as the common term, in Britain, for this third area. It allows an expansion of the day-to-day usage which professionals assign it. Design, in its most general educational sense, can be defined as the area of experience, skill and understanding that reflects appreciation and adaption of people's surrounding in the light of both material and spiritual needs.

Is Design or even small "d" design developed enough to demand parity with Science and Humanities in the school system? Is there sufficient knowledge of the nature of design skills, ability and "ways of knowing?" Do we know enough about the design process in the individual to enable judgment to be made as to methods of teaching and organization of relevant material?

The literature review conducted for the **Ideabook** unearthed no texts that clearly explain fundamental ideas, concepts and processes with particular application to Design. The "fugitive" literature, especially proceedings from conferences, yielded some information that gives beginning teachers an understanding of teaching concepts and tried and tested methods of teaching -- supported by relevant research data. The **Architecture Education Study** (1981) provides some of this information but it is not easily accessible in a readily formulated theory form. The interviews for ideas yielded useful teaching methods but rarely were they in a theory form or supported by research.

It is difficult to define design as an area of knowledge. To compete with other subjects in a school system, it must contribute to an individual's self-realization and to preparation for social roles. Cross suggests this might be accomplished by providing instruction to concepts like problem solving, citizen action processes and improved environmental awareness, thereby showing the contribution design activities make to an individual's life and the lives of others.

This exploration has cited reasons for the non-existence of Design in our schools: the focus on career preparation, the lack of a usable body of knowledge in the same form as most other knowledge and the important point to identifying how it prepares one for "life." Due to these reasons, Design thinking and feeling does not begin early enough. Instead, students arrive at the university after twelve years of "formal" education (the 3Rs) plus the education process that goes on at home from birth. They have had little exposure to visual thinking processes. Even worse, this system of education both at home and school, has made them wary. They usually have been conditioned, unfortunately, by fear. In his book **How Children Fail**, John Holt is explicit about what radically changes that inherent desire and ability to learn found in infants. He believes, and I agree, that adults destroy this intellectual and creative capacity by:

> making children afraid of not doing what other people want, of not pleasing, of failing, or of being wrong. Thus we make them afraid to experiment, afraid to try the difficult and the unknown.[13]

Teachers, because they spend a great deal of time with students, are leaders in this scenario. Too often teachers themselves are afraid. They tend to deal with this lack of confidence and fragile sense of self-worth by "waging an endless psychological war against the children to make them even more insecure, anxious and fearful than they themselves."[14]

Students are so indoctrinated to this system that it is hard for them to become open to learning and willing to experiment. It is the instructor's role, in a design class, to re-ignite the interest in learning and allow expansion of the intellectual, explorative and visual thinking capacities of the student. Teachers must feel confident enough **not** to need to make students feel inadequate or insecure.

Design with a big "D" is a good place for early schooling to start. As research and publishing in the field of Design continues, its inclusion in the school system could help the problem of fear described by John Holt. The open-ended, issue as opposed to answer-centeredness, qualities that design should have do not recognize that same kind of failure. If Design were taught in schools, the job of the university design instructor would change radically. Students would arrive with some big "D" type thinking behind them -- teachers could truly become resource people.

design knowledge... what do we know about?

Julian Beinart, in his **Architecture Education Study** papers,[15] has summarized the work of several authors on design knowledge. Three ways to develop design theory are: verification/cycle research, integration and synthesis. Reasons are cited for the failure of these methods to systematically produce "knowledge." In cycle research, the reason given is the lack of testing mechanisms or ways to make solutions verifiable. But what about the post-occupancy evaluation (POE) technique? Students do not build buildings or spaces but they can go out and test the assumptions of other designs/designers and document the results of those tests. Several ideas on "verifiable" projects resulted from the interviews. Each design studio should have a mandate to test and document more theory.

The integration model is criticized because of "borrowing" from other disciplines; both Hillier and Musgrave argue that the design process (the analysis-synthesis model) is a misreading of the scientific model and does not really work for design. The crux of integrative ability would appear to be "clear thinking." Herein lies the importance of awareness about teaching thinking. The process described by de Bono (Chapter 2, C:ii), originally from studies of children, can be "borrowed" and applied to design to make the process of thinking clearer for design students. Borrowed theory need not necessarily be bad; it is the same as borrowed form in design. You do not have to be original -- you have to be "clear."

One of the clearest and most useful borrowing of theory for design comes from the natural and behavioral sciences. How do behavioral and natural sciences meet, co-exist and flourish in the design learning setting? I think they are the basis for the body of knowledge or theories that we are searching for as the framework for design. They must be part of the studio as the hard facts and principles; they contribute information about people and the environment. The key is to educate the "studio" teacher to these sciences so they are a part of his/her natural mode of operations and become part of every studio project. Another key is access to this "science" information -- through a resource center (computer in the future) where students can quickly find answers in the form of principles and theories that are useful to them. Through each step we must continue compiling, researching and documenting our designs. Design studios should teach how to document theories from our designs.

I believe design knowledge does exist, however the question of how we teach this knowledge is closer to the heart of the **Ideabook**. At present, from literature review and idea interviews, we teach randomly, sometimes with little regard to **how** people learn. The powerful ideas are usually linked to a learning theory, e.g., sufficient wait time means that the brain needs time to process information. It is not mysterious -- theories do exist on how we learn and they are often applicable to design learning.

perspectives... where to look?

There are many places to look for different perspectives on design education, e.g., fields such as music or drama. How do you teach music? Composition? Conducting? How to play the piano? There are basic skills, techniques and theories; there is also interpretation, emotions and feelings. In music schools they **teach** the skills and provide examples and a comfortable environment in which to **develop** the interpretation. Learning music and design have elements in common. Temperaments matter, but so does skill; frustrations abound, but the rewards of "break through" make it worthwhile. Analyzing the "how" of learning another field could help the "how" of learning design. Design practicing and learning appears to be less rigorous than the scales, arpeggios and techniques or cadences, form and music theory of music learning. However, design is no less a mind/body coordination than playing the piano. Are design routines needed for warm-up? Drawing exercises often do that -- but do they warm up the mind? Perhaps spatial exercises are necessary. Perspective exploration leads to a variety of design teaching ideas.

Another perspective is that design education should be conservation. Neil Postman in **Teaching as a Conserving Activity** maintains that most systems are slow to change; perhaps this is fortunate. He says that our culture is overdosing on change and that the function of education is to provide some stability and a counter-argument to that change. This thermostatic view suggests that culture should keep its outlook steady and balanced in an ecological sense. Postman's position is that education is a problem of conservation -- not growth. Schools should become an agency in society with no vested interest in change itself. They would then become responsive to the information biases of culture and provide a balance to these biases. He says that what is most relevant to students is that which the information or media environment (the non-school environment) fails to provide them. What is really relevant is what culture is insisting is irrelevant. A good example is language. An information environment which does not stress language and language development must be countered by an education that does. What are the implications for design education? Are we thermostatically responsive to the information environment? Postman suggests a way that this responsiveness can take place by emphasizing **history** as our most potent intellectual means of achieving a raised consciousness.

> Every subject should be taught as history, setting the stage in human development with a past and a future.[16]

What does this say about our design curriculum? Do we focus enough on giving the basis of design in the setting of history and giving the thermostatic view of the media environment?

If design education is for conservation or as a balance check then design schools should be pursuing what the profession is not. One might argue that when students leave this conservation system he/she will be unprepared for the little "d" design world. Theoretically, this new schooling, grounded in history and overall perspective, prepares the student for anything and everything -- like the classical education tradition. If TV teaches only what is new and changing, who or what will teach what is old, stable and the foundations of our culture?

Another perspective: are designers best educated as generalists or specialists? The battle continues between education in breadth and education in depth. Generally, the curricula for schools is a compromise between the two doctrines. Horst Rittel points out the weakness of another option -- breadth vs. width where width is a long list of electives or prerequisites for students that are mutually unrelated introductions to various fields. Rittel questions the capability of the student to synthesize these bits and pieces. He maintains that specialists often forget to question the foundations of their specialty as they are entrenched as members of a small sub-culture. This results in the criticism of narrow-mindedness directed to the specialists.[17, 18]

The generalist/specialist issue in education appears to be one of inter-connectedness and usefulness of the breadth offerings. It might be said that generalists and specialists are born, not made. Some people easily focus in on one small area, acclimatize and happily explore that territory. Others need the wide open spaces of the generalist philosophy. In design, we need both.

design education models...

The interviews unearthed few new studio "formats" that vary from the traditional approach. The **Architecture Education Study** discussed the evolution of the academic tradition of teaching design from the apprenticeship system to the Beaux Arts method of separating design from other studies. This encouraged designers to be concerned with formal images and, along with the economics of architecture, to attend to largely privileged clients. **AES** cites three movements which have attempted to modify this approach: the methodologist (application of mathematical models to relieve the designer's dependence on intuition in design decisions), the advocates (formed advocacy groups to represent the concerns of minority groups) and the sociologists (studied individual and social behavior to provide an empirical base for design decisions).

> But (none of these movements) generated models powerful enough to supersede the studio approach to teaching design; the inscrutible character of design and its teaching continued.[19]

Why **does** the traditional mode persist? People need good reasons to make changes; changes take time, energy, investment and generally include an element of risk. Teachers and administrators are extremely busy people. To revamp a system that has been entrenched in most universities since their beginnings is a time consuming task -- especially for in-house faculty. It would mean documenting what is **wrong** with the existing studio format. In summary, the traditional model advocates that the mastery of the teacher is communicated through demonstration and criticism at the student's desk. Problems with this model can be itemized. Students find it difficult to evaluate the strongly espoused but divergent ideas and knowledge which is imparted by design teachers. They also perceive the different nature of design knowledge, yet do not understand the implications through their studio experience. Students must deal with ambiguous and often incomplete communication, leaving them confused about what design is and how they are ever going to find out. The studio model emphasizes practice, educational systems devoted to practice become limited in their ability to accumulate knowledge systematicaly (**AES**, Beinart).

These problems would have to be well documented with factual evidence for administrations and faculty alike to consider changing the old model. A new model would have to solve at least some of these difficulties. Such a model will have to be based on principles like the following:

1. Teacher as resource person, not "master."

2. A developed, documented body of knowledge or theory that is a teachable/learnable part of the design curriculum.

3. A commitment to responding to social needs in society, not just traditional priviledged clients.

4. An emphasis on communication skills within the design community; awareness of espoused and in-use theories of behavior.

5. A commitment to exploring ideologies and values that form the basis for design.

6. A program to make the way of teaching and learning not just devoted to practice but also a part of accumulating knowledge about design.

Some of these principles are in use in the Advocacy Models in Chapter 3, although too often these studios lack the structure of a knowledge base and an adequately developed sense of behavioral dynamics.

How can talk be turned to action? One response is to hire a consultant to observe the studio, to analyze the curriculum and do the busy and thinking work to help the faculty and administration make decisions regarding the future of design education programs. Such a consultant would need experience as a designer, an educator and an organizer -- it is a new niche for the designer/educator.

teaching roles and styles...

star designer or armchair analyst?

Roles are the characteristics and expected social behavior of an individual. Teachers can take on many roles: information giver, modeler of thought processes, referrer, motivator, evaluator, planner or disciplinarian. In teaching design the teaching role usually extends to be a professional role model. It is the responsibility of a teacher to have a commitment to a set of beliefs that are reflected in what they say and in their day-to-day operations of both teaching and designing. In the design process, human values, role models and knowledge systems all, to some degree, structure a student's design activities. Peter Burgess in his article "Political Knowledge and the Architecture Studio"[20] suggests three role models: egoist, pragmatist and facilitator. The chart on page 116 takes these models and expands them to include sub-groups and typical characteristics.

Role models have many connections. Tom Bartuska[21] has connnected Piaget's cognitive development theory, through the work of Lawrence Kohlberg on moral development, to roles. (See his article for more details because the combination of roles and values is valuable to observe.) We can see the connection between understanding developmental psychology (Piaget) and how that understanding is manifested in human values and teaching roles (see chart on page 117).

From the literature review it is clear we are gradually shifting to a version of Koh's[22] holistic ecological designer. Architect Tom Bartuska supports this opinion by suggesting an ecological approach to architecture. He refers to ecology as a unifying influence supported by theories such as functionalism (how design fits context), levels of integration theory, territoriality and defensible space (themes of human ecology), energy and the health, fitness and creativity model (McHarg). Bartuska lists other concepts which also fit into and strengthen the ecological model: Christopher Alexander's **A Pattern Language**, contextual studies, indigenous architecture, life-cycle cost analysis, environmental policy acts and Buckminster Fuller's synergy concepts. Bartuska goes so far as to say that this ecological approach could well be the unifying theme of the architecture profession in the 80's as it has been to the landscape architectural profession in the 70's.

Koh pushes the ecological notion farther by adding the modifier "holistic," emphasizing the importance of the whole and the interdependence of its parts. I like the fact that this holism implies, as Koh writes:

> The act of designing/building cannot be appropriately explained, designed and evaluated without reference to physical, biological, cultural and psychological environments.[23]

This relates directly to the theory base for design: natural and behavioral sciences with theories that we test and rewrite in our own language. But there is little new in what Koh has to say. McHarg was on to it in the 70's; the shift is evolving slowly.

Behind the teaching role is style, the **way** in which something is said or done -- the combination of distinctive qualities of imagination and individuality expressed in actions. According to Kenneth Eble:

> Style is as important as character for the aspiring teacher. Customary academic behaviors may get in the way of developing both. Personality is an important fact in any common sense notion of teaching. (Kenneth Eble, **Improving Teaching Styles**, 1980)

Teaching styles are connected to effectiveness. As a teacher, examine your own teaching style and behavior to allow growth and change when needed. Help is readily available on most campuses to undertake such an evaluation.

Behind the role and style is how you actually perceive yourself. This has a great affect on how you teach. If a teacher feels joyful about his/her work and transmits that feeling to their thinking, actions and approach to students, the teaching is more effective. If you do feel "passion" about what you do, designing or teaching, this is a privileged position. The problem then is to have compassion for those who lack your passion (Lars Lerup in conservation).

designer/teacher roles

role model	characteristics	teaching approach

egoist
- STAR DESIGNER — "give 'em what I want"... instructor is studio master & critic
- MOVEMENT LEADER — "I know what is good for them"... policy making
- WORKER/PUBLIC SERVANT — corporate design production... Look, see, copy, don't think

pragmatist
- ENTREPRENEUR — economy conscious but keep status quo... professional practice
- ENGINEER/TECHNOLOGIST — solving problems with technical solutions & facts
- BUILDER/CONTRACTOR — in 'control', emphasis on practical knowledge

facilitator
- SOCIAL/ECONOMIC PROGRAMMER — guide people to make informed decisions
- COMMUNITY ADVOCATE — designer part of community who is client & user
- VALUE-INFORMED PROBLEM SOLVER — encourage social reform through design
- HOLISTICAL ECOLOGIST — design as evolutionary – ecological & social, instructor as co-worker & co-ordinator

theoretician
- ARTIST — design as irrational, intuitive process, emphasis on creative process
- CRAFTSPERSON — concern for technique & product, instructor as master
- CONTEXTUALIST — see all as social/cultural context, emphasis on cultural landscape
- ARMCHAIR ANALYST — writes & thinks, rarely builds, theoretical & philosophical

116

value continuum... attitudes and roles

Bartuska: p. 130

DETERMINANTS OF HUMAN VALUES	SIX STAGES OF MORAL DEVELOPMENT	FORM AND FUNCTION	ATTITUDES	ROLES
PRE-CONVENTIONAL				
0-4 years hedonistic devotion to pleasure	punishment	function follows form	Masochistic: "Face it, make it work and to hell with the impact"	entrepreneur engineer/technologist
0-9 years pre-moral	hedonistic		Egotistical: maximum personal gain: "I want to do my own thing"	star designer movement leader
CONVENTIONAL				
10 years + system of social rule for majority of population	good/nice	form follows function	Style: keeping up with Jones "I did it because its in vogue"	worker public servant
	law & order		Functional: (physical sciences) societal laws & codes, technological & economical efficiency	builder/contractor
POST-CONVENTIONAL				
self-determined value system	social/humanistic	form and function are one	Social Purpose: (human sciences) equality and user participation	value-informed problem solver
	universal		Synergy: (ecological sciences) synthesis of social & environmental context	holistic ecological

mystery and mastery... who can solve it?

Demystify the learning process. School has tended to make students aware of an unknown force which makes teachers respond positively to the "right" and negatively to the "wrong." This answer-centered attitude does not work in the design studio. It closes off options. But students have been conditioned that right answers pay off and that the way to get ahead is to provide them. Teachers must be aware themselves of the difference between issue and answer-centeredness. It is reflected in the design school adage: We want to see process, not product. This is easy to say but far more difficult to follow through within a total philosophy. It is hard to judge process and thinking, hard to hang it up on the wall and admire it.

Demystify the design process itself. In the experiential studio setting students are expected to acquire competence mysteriously on their own. There is no tradition of scholarship that makes design somewhat "public" and therefore explicit. There is a mystique behind the designs in our environment. There are no clear answers written at the bases of buildings saying why they are like they are. There are no clear messages as to why the paving is brick or the trees are placed in rows. Designers do not explain their theories of "why" in literature. Therefore, the same mystique that prevents students from being prepared for competent practice also prohibits learning among design professionals. We must begin to document our experiences. Teachers have a responsibility to clearly explain the design process, to encourage students to practice it, get closer to it and work with it. Although there is little "written" theory, there is enough to build on and if explicitly stated there should be enough to "demystify" the activity.

Demystify creativity. There is emphasis on the study of creativity as applied to problem solving and specifically design education. Alon Kvashney defines creative behavior as the "production and the use of ideas both new and valuable to the creator."[24] Is creativity the same as innovation? My concern is that the inventive or original solution is not always the most valid or appropriate for a specific design or problem solving task. We must take care or define our notion of creativity to students -- as being different from originality. It is far more useful to be able to think clearly and laterally than only "originally." Too often students are encouraged to "be creative" and are given the message, sometimes unconsciously, that their work and by association they themselves are "insignificant" if the work is not unusual, different or unique. As teachers we can nurture the urge in all people to learn and create but we need not push everyone to be original.

Chris Argyris[25] observed student dependence on instructors -- the mystery behind design becomes synonymous with mastery of design. Especially in the push for originality students become desperate to find the key to the mystery that will bring about the mastery. The cycle returns to behavioral dynamics and the gap between espoused theories and theories in use. Until these inconsistencies are corrected the mystery/mastery syndrome will go on. There is a connection between professional effectiveness and the ideas presented in Chapter 3 which urge clear communication and response.

B. WHAT NEXT?

commentary

Design Education is a big topic. By concentrating on the techniques and "how-to" aspects, the topic is more manageable. But threads of significance are still attached to the why and what of design learning that are difficult to ignore. Design Education remains a big topic.

The research approach to this project is eclectic, rather than the hypothesis-research-conclusioos model. Two ways of describing the subject of ideas for how to teach were used: literature and ideas from practicing teachers. The eclectic model supports the contention that there are limits to the purely rational analysis of a problem. It subscribes to the theory of holistic ecological design: "There is an intrinsic limit to validity of the objective observation and scientific diagnosis of the (environmental) design problem." (Koh, p. 80) Resolving a direction and evolving theories of design education fulfills the minimum criteria as a challenging design problem.

The practical nature of a how-to **Ideabook** is difficult to mesh with a topic like design. **Short Cuts** and **Ideas That Work** are an attempt to attend to this practical requirement. I tried to continually ask the question: is this usable for the beginning design teacher? **Big Ideas** addresses the connection of this practical experience to the bigger issues in design education.

Short Cuts began as an extended annotated bibliography but grew into a study of key ideas supported by best references. This focusing approach is valuable for a busy teacher trying to broaden his/her background within a time limit. The literature review yielded key theories and ideas for Chapter 3. The topics of philosophy, psychology and general education are well covered in the literature; the difficulty is finding the most up-to-date "best" reference. Design education does not have this problem. The most useful sources are the fugitive literature. The **AES** is a beginning; it at least combines research and analysis in two volumes. **Short Cuts**, too, is a beginning. It is not intended to cover every key idea or reference, but instead presents an overview.

In conclusion, after this process of research and analysis, some beliefs about design education are summarized as follows:

There **is** a strong connection between theories in the fields of psychology, philosophy and education and **how** we teach design. Knowledge of the theories and observation of good design teachers allows one to see these theories in action. Like general teachers, design teachers should be trained and educated -- not just as designers but as teachers. Our graduate design programs need a strong education option so designer/teachers can avail themselves of educational theories and then apply them to design education. Schools are able to do much more theory building than at present. It should be mandatory that each year schools publish a book of works and theories that emerged through the year. These could be compiled, edited and bound to continue building the basis for design knowledge.

There **is** a communication problem in design education. Poor communication exists among people in general but is magnified in a fuzzy area like design. This quality of fuzziness or mystery has allowed both instructors and professionals to hide. A course is needed (for students and teachers) in behavior dynamics and communication skills. Application of the concepts from Argyris and Schon's **Theory in Practice** will facilitate a move from the defensive, unilateral control position of Model I to the minimally defensive, collaborator, facilitator role of Model II. This course is also needed by professionals to improve their communication skills.

There must be a social conscience behind design which infiltrates content and form; it guides both what and how we teach. It also guides how we define ourselves as people and designers. The way we teach has an effect on what students perceive and believe. This means that teaching some form of social conscience is part of our mandate.

research and exploration

Designers/design educators are rarely trained as researchers nor do they have the time or inclination to be engaged in empirical studies in humanistic, social or natural science disciplines. But they do have questions that can be answered through this type of research. For instance the very basic "learning about learning" research will occur in the discipline of psychology. The key ideas in **Short Cuts** are all subjects of continuing research and exploration in the related disciplines of philosophy, psychology, sociology and education. We are motivated to study design and the problem solving process to understand more fully how people think and to determine how to help them design better. We need to encourage interdisciplinary research that combines the skills and knowledge of the psychologist or sociologist with the designer and his/her process. The research will then apply directly to design but will no doubt discover other more general issues of interest to the related disciplines. Designers must recognize their limits in undertaking "research" without the background experience and training necessary. This points to the need for a designer/researcher with emphasis, energy commitment and training focused on the "researcher" aspect -- creating an important interdisciplinary niche. Schools should be encouraging people to explore these niches that are formed by connections with related disciplines and offer assistance in constructing programs that concentrate on the research mode. The field is too large to expect all designers to be good at or to like research.

This calls for a degree of specialization in key research areas. These areas are large topics to which I have added some specific design interest questions:

PHILOSOPHY

What are the connections between design and political ideologies? How can we better understand the social ethics base for how we design and teach?

PSYCHOLOGY

Is there more to know about developmental psychology of the young adult? Is learning to design different from other learning? How can designers learn more about learning? Is creativity teachable? Is thinking teachable? How? Can we know more about group dynamics in the design setting?

EDUCATION

Are general teaching techniques applicable directly to design education? What kinds of knowledge apply to design?

Motivations to research and explore are found in the **Ideabook** interview comments and in design literature. They point to the need for theories to understand and thus teach design better. Theories are not mystical discoveries but are built piece by piece to form the foundations or the definition of a particular subject. As discussed in **Big Ideas**, design requires these basic foundations. The sources of our design knowledge are experience, reflection (exploration) and systematic research. It is our job to explore cycle research, theory borrowing and synthesis models of designing. It is our job to look back in history for theoretical design principles and to analyze and test them in practice and in the design education setting. Design research and explorations must be an integral part of the training and education of designers. A cooperative effort to build the theoretical foundations of design will involve:

1. DOCUMENTING the design experience, every design experience, in an analytical way -- trying to understand and communicate the "whys" of designing. Each project, large or small, should be written up with a storyline explaining in plain language, experiences, process, product and conclusions. An attempt must be made to hypothesize theories and connect ideas to present and past experiences.

2. PUBLISHING these works so other designers/educators can learn, copy, modify and therefore contribute their own explorations.

3. RECOGNIZING both scientific **research** and subjective **explorations** as valid contributions to design knowledge. Magazines such as **Design Methods Journal** and **Design Studies** need to attract a larger readership by including research, exploration and commentary.

The following are explorations as extensions of the **Ideabook**.

1. IDEABOOK RESOURCE NETWORK.

The **Ideabook** has been written with a view of expansion. With more time, money and energy, the process of collecting ideas, by interview or questionnaire, can continue. A more complete version, including information from more interviews will provide more specific useful ideas. Ideally, the **Ideabook** will become part of an educational resource network on a computer system. With this framework each design school can contribute new ideas with immediate accessibility by other network "users." This kind of resource system will encompass both ideas, an annotated bibliography and a project file. The whole system can be keyworded to be most useful as a quick and easy reference.

2. START A COURSE CALLED "BEHAVIORAL DYNAMICS FOR DESIGNERS" and learn to speak, listen and teach Model II language.

If there is a discrepancy between what students say they do when designing and what they in fact do (espoused and theories in use) where do they learn this behavior and how can they re-learn a more congruent behavior?

An inquiry into behavioral dynamics in the design studio will involve case studies observing the "theories in practice" of students and professors. A specific set of experiments will compare what people say and think and what they in fact do. This often is an example of what Argyris and Schon call "incongruent behavior" (Model I) which we generally learn from our parents and other social settings where the learning process is based on a reward/punishment system. In Model II or effective learning behavior the individual internalizes and tests the new behavior making it part of him/her if it is satisfying. Assuming Model I is deepseated in most of us -- how do we shift to the more effective Model II? This transition can happen through making students and teachers aware of their behavior and exploring and applying group dynamics of learning. The goal would be to design a learning environment according to Model II. This is a complex situation: Students struggle and question the validity of Model II and the teacher finds him/herself in the position of being successful when students express feelings and in fact confront the teacher.

A course on shifting from Model I to Model II, based on the work of Argyris and Schon but modified for designers, would help teachers and students alike. This type of course would support studio activities by allowing issues to be open for examination and teach us to specifically think, speak and listen in "Model II."

3. MAKE EXPLICIT CONNECTIONS BETWEEN GENERAL LEARNING THEORIES AND SPECIFIC DESIGN LEARNING TECHNIQUES.

Observing how general theories are translated, generally, unconsciously, to design learning would involve observation in design studios and the creation of a typology for the theory connectors. This research will explore the cognitive field approach as applicable to design teaching.

What next? Documentation of design education research and exploration will hopefully continue and increase. Each design instructor has a responsibility to report on the research that actually is their teaching. New approaches, ideas and observations evolve out of practicing the teaching/learning process. Share the wealth.

endnotes

[1] Josuck Koh, "Ecological Design: A Post Modern Design Paradigm of Holistic Philosophy and Evolutionary Ethic." Landscape Journal, Fall, 1982, p. 76.

[2] Ibid., p. 77.

[3] Ibid., p. 79.

[4] Randy Pierce and Mike Martin, "As if Students Mattered: Some Intellectual and Motivational Premises." ACSA 1979, p. 24.

[5] Ibid., p. 24.

[6] Ibid., p. 30.

[7] Morris Bigge, **Learning Theories for Teachers** (New York: Harper and Row, 1982), p. 325.

[8] Michael Jordan, "A Summary of Research on Introductory Design Education." Proceedings of 67th ACSA Annual Meeting, July 1979.

[9] Robert McKim, **Experiences in Visual Thinking** (Belmont: Wadsworth Publishing, 1972), p. 24.

[10] Anita Cross, "Design and General Education." **Design Studies** Vol. 1, No. 4 (April 1980), pp. 202-206.

[11] Bruce Archer, "Design as Discipline -- the 3Rs." **Design Studies**, Vol. 1, No. 1 (1979), p. 20.

[12] Ibid., p. 20.

[13] John Holt, **How Children Fail** (New York: Dell, 1982), p. 274.

[14] Ibid., p. 281.

[15] Julian Beinart, "Structure of the Content of Design." AES (Cambridge: MIT Press, 1981).

[16] Neil Postman, **Teaching as a Conserving Activity** (New York: Dell, 1979), p. 147.

[17] Horst Rittel, "Some Principles for the Design of an Educational System for Design." **Education for Architectural Technology**, April 1966, p. 12.

[18]Ibid., p. 13.

[19]**Architecture Education Study** (Cambridge: MIT Press, 1981), p. xi.

[20]Peter Burgess, "Political Knowledge and the Architecture Studio." **JAE,** Vol. 34, No. 3, Spring 1981, pp. 24-28.

[21]Tom Bartuska, "Values, Architecture and Context: The Emergence of an Ecological Approach to Architecture and the Built Environment." **ACSA,** 1981, pp. 128-134.

[22]Jusuck Koh, "Ecological Design: A Post Modern Design Paradigm of Holistic Philosophy and Evolutionary Ethic." **Landscape Journal,** Fall, 1982, p. 77.

[23]Ibid., p. 80.

[24]Alon Kvashney, "Enhancing Creativity in Landscape Architectural Education." **Landscape Journal,** Vol. 1, No. 2, Fall, 1982, p. 108.

[25]Chris Argyris, "Teaching and Learning in Design Settings." **AES,** 1981.

books

Adams, William, 1980. **The Experience of Teaching and Learning.** Seattle: Psychological Press. 165 pages.

Axelrod, J., 1964. **The University Teacher as an Artist: Toward an Aesthetics of Teaching with Emphasis on the Humanities.** San Francisco: Jossey-Bass. 246 pages.

This book is a detailed study of the dynamics of the college and university class, full of anecdotes about the effects on student learning on what a teacher does or does not do. The most interesting aspect was the portraits of various "prototypes" of teachers and the discussion on the changing attitudes to students as well as the reactions of the "system" through the 60's, 70's and 80's.

Bannister, T. S., 1954. **The Architect at Mid-Century: Evolution and Achievement.** New York: Reinhold Publishing Corporation. Volume I. 345 pages.

Bannister edited this report of the Commission for the Survey of Education and Registration for the AIA in 1954.

Beard, Ruth M. and Donald A. Bligh, 1971. **Research into Teaching Methods in Higher Education.** London: Society for Research into Higher Education. Third Edition. 104 pages.

This book summarizes the findings of British research into the processes of learning, and methods of teaching which are conducive to learning at university levels. The notes are grouped under main headings: aims and objectives, economy and efficiency, recall and retention of information, skills and abilities, teaching for change of attitudes, and evaluation of students, teachers and teaching methods. There are numerous references and a good index.

Berte, N. R. (Editor), 1975. **Individualizing Education: New Directions for Higher Education.** San Francisco: Jossey-Bass. 103 pages.

Editor Berte defines learning contracts as "Written agreements between a student and a faculty member or committee regarding a particular amount of student work and the institutional reward or credit for this work." This source book discusses this process of individualizing education for students -- both the philosophical rational and the practical realities of various approaches. Chapters of interest are John Duley's "Out of Class Contract Learning at Justin Morrill" and Berte's "Bringing About Change in a Traditional University."

Bigge, Morris L., 1982. **Learning Theories for Teachers.** New York: Harper and Rowe. Fourth Edition. 356 pages.

This text gives a clear overall picture of modern learning theories. It is easy to read and informative. See **Short Cuts** (Chapter 2: **Ideabook**)

Biggs, Donald A., Charles J. Palvino and Carlton E. Beck, 1976. **Counseling and Values.** Washington: American Personnel and Guidance Association. 383 pages.

Bligh, Donald A., 1972. **What's the Use of Lectures?** Hertfordshire, England: Penguin Books.

Bloom, Benjamin S. (Editor), 1956. **Taxonomy of Educational Objectives: Cognitive Domain.** New York: David McKay Co., Inc. 207 pages.

Brameld, Theodore B., 1956. **Toward a Reconstructed Philosophy of Education.** New York: Dryden. 417 pages.

Cohen, Uriel and John Hunter, 1981. **Teaching Design for Mainstreaming the Handicapped.** Milwaukee: University of Wisconsin, School of Architecture and Urban Planning. Report R81-1.

Consortium of East Coast School of Architecture, 1981. **Architecture Education Study - The Papers #1.** Cambridge MA: Massachusetts Institute of Technology Press. 851 pages.

A great resource of studio experiences, in the form of case studies. Along with Volume 2 which analyzes two of the studios in greater depth, highly recommended reading for both educator and practitioner.

Consortium of East Coast Schools of Architecture, 1981. **Architecture Education Study - The Cases #2.** Cambridge, MA: MIT Press. 560 pages.

In-depth analysis of two design studio case studies - highly recommended in conjunction with Volume 1's broader collection of studio study papers.

Coulter, Charles W. and Richard S. Rimanoczy, 1955. **A Layman's Guide to Educational Theory.** New York: D. Van Nostrand Co., Inc. 159 pages.

This is an interesting, easy to read book with a simple layout of graphic charts and newspaper-like headlines. Coulter comments: "Perhaps this is bad literary practice, but it (the format) is based on the well-known headlines consciousness of the American reading public." The book is a study of inventions of educational theories -- why they arose and what they meant to society at the time.

Cudnohufsky, Walter, 1979. **Working Paper #1: Comments on Design Education.** Conway, MA: Conway School of Landscape Design Inc.

Cudnohufsky, Walter, 1979. **Working Paper #3: Comments on Design Education.** Conway, MA: Conway School of Landscape Design Inc.

Cudnohufsky, Walter and Asheley Griffith, 1979. **Working Paper #2: Improving L.A. Education: Recommendation for a New Design.** Conway, MA: Conway School of Landscape Design Inc.

Davis, James R., 1976. **Teaching Strategies for the College Classroom.** Boulder, CO: Westview Press. 136 pages.

This book divides into four strategies: 1) Employing instructional systems. 2) Communicating through lectures. 3) Facilitating inquiry. 4) Utilizing group processes. There is a good section on choosing and using a teaching strategy and a bibliographical essay on various books about college teaching which is very useful.

de Bono, Edward, 1969, **The Mechanism of Mind.** New York: Simon and Schuster. 275 pages.

In the first half of the book the organization of the brain is put together step by step. The second half shows how the mechanism actually works in practice and how it only works in certain ways. Four basic types of thinking are described: natural, logical, mathematical and lateral. "The first part deals with the beauty of function, of process and organization. The second part deals directly with how the brain thinks, how people think." I enjoyed this book very much. de Bono uses examples to explain his ideas. Sample quote from page 279: "If information is the door that gives access to the world, then emotion is not just the paint on the door but the handle with which the door is opened."

de Bono, Edward, 1976. **Teaching Thinking.** London: Maurice Temple Smith. 238 pages.

de Bono's book is a clear explanation of his view of the thinking process and how it should be taught. He espouses a program called CORT, in which the traditional abstraction process in a thinking situation is bypassed by using tools that are deliberately created for the purpose. Each CORT lesson is based on one of the tools. Easy to read and interesting.

Dressel, Paul L. and Nellie T. Hardy, 1977. **College Teaching as a Profession.** East Lansing: Michigan State University. 156 pages.

This publication discusses four teaching approaches: student-centered and instructor-centered (affective), discipline-centered and instructor-centered. "Teachers at best are mediators and expediters of learning."

Dressel, Paul L. and Sally B. Pratt, 1971. **The World of Higher Education: An Annotated Guide to the Major Literature.** San Francisco: Jossey-Bass, 238 pages.

Dye, Allan and Harold Hackney, 1975. **Gestalt Approaches to Counseling.** Boston: Houghton Mifflin Co. 74 pages.

Eble, Ken (Editor), 1980. **Improving Teaching Styles: New Directors for Teaching and Learning #1.** San Francisco: Jossey-Brass, Inc. 107 pages.

This source book attempts to probe some of the mysteries of style through articles that define teaching style, give examples of distinctive styles and suggest ways in which style may be acquired and put to good use. The last few chapters emphasize working with behaviors of teachers -- with attention to how to help teachers change some of their behaviors. Axelrod's chapter on tracing the changing styles of a professor from 1959-1984 was interesting as were the chapters by John Granrose on "Conscious Teaching" and the Ishlers' chapter on "A Strategy for Developing Desirable Teaching Behavior."

Eble, Kenneth, 1972. **Professors as Teachers.** San Francisco: Jossey-Bass. 202 pages.

This book reflects Professor Eble's thoughts and conclusions resulting from many visits to campuses across the USA. He describes college teaching as he found it -- conventional. His chapter on evaluating teaching is a good one. He favors student evaluation of teaching, conscious preparation of graduate students for teaching their subjects, systematic, though informal, in-service staff development programs and the improvement of the conditions in and under which teaching and learning take place.

Eble, Kenneth, 1976. **The Craft of Teaching.** San Francisco: Jossey-Bass. 179 pages.

Teaching is treated as a craft in which one's performance can be bettered through attention to detail. Following a short overview of popular assumptions and teaching attitudes and skills, Eble discusses teaching in and out of the classroom, and the problem of practical day-to-day teaching. A final section deals with the preparation of teachers in graduate school, and the attitudes which result. This book provides both useful and specific practical ideas from an expert.

Feyerabend, Paul, 1975. **Against Method: Outline of an Anarchistic Theory of Knowledge.** Atlantic Highlands, NJ: Humanities Press.

Feyerabend states that his intention is to convince the reader that "all methodologies, even the most obvious ones, have their limits." He maintains that science is essentially an anarchistic enterprise and that theoretical anarchism is more humanitarian and more likely to encourage progress than its law and order alternatives. He works on the premise that the only principle that does not inhibit progress is: ANYTHING GOES . . . in other words by proceeding "counter-inductively." I liked his attitude to research.

Fountain, Charles A., 1965. **Landscape Architecture: Education and the Profession.** Berkeley: MLA Thesis. 188 pages.

The purpose of this thesis is to familiarize the reader with the nature and scope of landscape architecture and to determine the need for extending professional training in the field. Special attention is given to the possibility of instruction at small colleges. The thesis contains one of the rare pieces of writing on the history of landscape architecture education.

Frazier, Craig and John Zeisel (Editors), 1974. **Teaching Man-Environment Relations: Selected Techniques, EDRA 5 Workshop.** Milwaukee, WI: EDRA Arch. Res. Office, GSD, Harvard.

This booklet is a compilation of descriptions of "special, successful or innovative teaching techniques" and "innovative curricular structures" in the field of Person-Environment Relations in Schools of Design and Behavioral Sciences. It formed part of the teaching session at EDRA 5 in 1974. It suggests some good techniques and ideas for teaching.

Freire, Paulo, 1968. **Pedagogy of the Oppressed.** New York: Seabury.

Gagne, R. M. and L. J. Briggs, 1974. **Principles of Industrial Design.** New York: Holt, Rinehart and Winston. 270 pages.

This book is intended to assist teachers who have responsibility for planning instructional programs. The author reviews basic processes of learning and instruction, designing instruction, and instructional systems.

Gagne, Robert, 1975. **Essentials of Learning for Instruction, Principles of Educational Psychology.** Hinsdale, IL: Dryden Press. 204 pages.

This book includes the basic facts and principles for teaching. Non-threatening and easy to read, it serves well as a framework for organizing thoughts and teaching knowledge.

Gagne, Robert, 1977. **The Conditions of Learning.** New York: Holt, Rinehart and Winston. Third Edition. 407 pages.

This book is intended for students of psychology and education, and makes references to educational problems. The author notes that learning must be linked to the design of instruction - considering the different capabilities involved. The book deals thoroughly with types and forms of learning and problem solving.

Gullette, Margaret Morganroth (Editor), 1982. **The Art and Craft of Teaching.** Cambridge, MA: Havard-Danforth Center for Teaching and Learning.

Highet, G., 1959, **The Art of Teaching.** New York: Knopf Publishing. 289 pages.

A somewhat dated book on teaching methods - including lecturing, tutoring, recitation and punishment. The chapter on Great Teachers and Their Pupils: Socrates, Jesus, etc., is of interest.

Hilgard, Ernest and Gordon Bower, 1966. **Theories of Learning.** New York: Meredith Publishing Co. 661 pages.

This is a classic text on learning theory -- updated in 1966, running through Thorndike's Connectionism, Pavlov's Classical Conditioning, Skinner's Operant Conditioning, Gestalt Theory, Freud's Psychodynamics, Information Processing Models, etc. -- more than you ever need to know on learning theory -- and not as easy to read as Bigge.

Hills, Philip, 1979. **Teaching and Learning as a Communication Process.** New York: Halsted Press. 128 pages.

Hollander, Edwin P. and Raymond G. Hunt (Editors), 1963. **Current Perspectives in Social Psychology.** New York: Oxford University Press. 590 pages.

Holt, John, 1982. **How Children Fail.** New York: Dell Publishing. Second Edition. 298 pages.

Holt's book originated from a series of memos written to a colleague about a fifth grade class he observed and taught. The first section "Strategy" deals with the ways in which children try to meet, or dodge the demands that adults make of them in school. "Fear and Failure," the second section, deals with the interaction in children of fear and failure, and the effect of this on strategy and learning. "Real Learning" is about the difference between what children appear to know or are expected to know, and what they really know. The last section "How School Fails" analyzes ways in which schools foster bad strategies, raise fears and produce fragmentary, often short-lived learning. They fail to meet the needs of children. The book is valuable in realizing the basic framework of education most of us went through and to consider how strongly it affects the teaching and learning at the university level today.

Institute of Advanced Architectural Studies, 1975. **Interim Report: Research Paper 6 Mid-Career Education for the Building Professions: A Study Related to Learning Needs.** York: University of York, Institute of Advanced Architectural Studies.

Institute of Advanced Architectural Studies, 1975. **Second Report: Research Paper 10 Mid-Career Education for the Building Professions: A Study of Learning Needs and Learning Styles.** York: University of York, Institute of Advanced Architectural Studies.

Kaplan, Abraham, 1964. **The Conduct of Inquiry.** San Francisco: Chandler Publishing Co. 428 pages.

Keleti, Peter, 1981. **Learning and Teaching the Craft of Architecture.** Kansas City: Published as a manuscript. 49 pages.

This publication addresses the learning and teaching of architecture in four parts. Chapter One discusses educational responsibility (public safety, self education and teaching). Chapter Two is about architectural philosophy and personal identify. Chapter Three discusses learning the craft and Chapter Four is about teaching the craft -- instructional objectives and structuring learning experience -- not easy to digest.

Kibler, Robert J., Donald J. Cegala, Larry L. Barker and David T. Miles, 1974. **Objectives for Instruction and Evaluation.** Boston: Allyn and Bacon, Inc. 203 pages.

This identifies the important functions that instructional objectives can serve in improving education. See **Short Cuts** (Chapter 2: **Ideabook**).

Knapper, C. K. (Editor), 1982. **Expanding Learning Through New Communication Technologies, New Directions for Teaching and Learning #9.** San Francisco: Jossey-Bass. 107 pages.

Editor Knapper makes the point that education -- especially teaching -- seems to remain remarkably impervious to technological change -- despite what is going on in the rest of our lives. This book describes a variety of technologies that are already affecting university teaching or will do so in the near future. Topics such as programmed learning, educational television or computer assisted instruction are NOT dealt with here. Instead the author concentrates on new technologies that are in the developmental stages such as videodiscs and videotex.

Kneller, George, 1971. **An Introduction to Philosophy of Education.** New York: John Wiley and Sons. Second Edition. 118 pages.

Krathwohl, David R., Benjamin S. Bloom and Bertram B. Basia, 1964. **Taxonomy of Educational Objectives: Affective Domain.** New York: David McKay Co., Inc. 196 pages.

Lancaster, Otis E., 1974. **Effective Teaching and Learning.** New York: Gordon and Breach. 385 pages.

This book is an outgrowth of fifteen annual two week seminars on effective teaching conducted by the author in the College of Engineering at Pennsylvania State University. The book is divided into: 1) objectives; 2) learning; and 3) a main section on methods and processes. The chapters on "Design Experience" and "Stimulating Creativity" are of special interest.

Mager, Robert, 1975. **Preparing Instructional Objectives.** Belmont, CA: Fearon Publishers. Second Edition. 60 pages.

A great little book for help in putting together course objectives. The book is written for busy people -- you are not meant to read the book page by page, but rather questions guide you to the specific information you require. It is laid out in a way which will help the reader attain the capabilities which are his/her reasons for reading the book.

Maslow, A. H., 1968. **Toward a Psychology of Being.** New York: Van Nostrand. 240 pages.

McGinty, Tim, 1979. **Best Beginning Design Projects: Submissions from Architecture Schools Around the U.S.** Milwaukee: WP79-5 Center for Architecture and Urban Planning Research. 111 pages.

McKeachie, W. J., 1978. **Teaching Tips: A Guidebook for the Beginning College Teacher.** Lexington and Toronto: D.C. Heath and Company. Seventh Edition. 280 pages.

Says McKeachie: "This is not a textbook in the Educational Psychology of College Teaching. It is merely a compilation of useful (occasionally mechanical) tricks of the trade which I, as a teacher, have found useful in running classes" (p. 1). There are chapters on preparing for courses, meeting a class for the first time, lecturing, organizing effective discussion, the psychology of learning, student ratings of faculty and "improving your teaching." Each offers advice and refers to relevant research findings.

McKim, Robert H., 1972. **Experiences in Visual Thinking.** Belmont, CA: Wadsworth Publishing Company. 171 pages.

Milton, Ohmer and Associates, 1978. **On College Teaching: A Guide to Contemporary Practices.** San Francisco: Josey-Bass. 403 pages.

A comprehensive text dealing with specific elements of teaching, addressed by one expert per chapter. Useful and interesting chapters include: Clarifying Objectives, Leading Discussions, Specifying and Achieving Competencies, Being There Vicariously by Case Studies, and Applying Gaming and Simulations. A favorite quote is, "Teachers open the door, you enter by yourself."

Moffett, M. S., 1975. **The Teaching of Design.** Cambridge: MIT, Ph.D. Thesis. 207 pages.

This thesis is an investigation of design teaching in architecture and mechanical engineering. Moffett proposes a definition of design along with generic issues relating to the evaluation and teaching activity in each field. The historical precedent in each field in described followed by a close look at the evolution of design subjects in the curricula of the two professions at MIT. A design class in each was observed, as case studies, over an entire semester. The thesis evolves a comparative analysis of the two cases. The major similarities were: 1) design was taught as problem solving; 2) design was taught through criticism of students' work and 3) design teaching involved simultaneous use of visual, verbal and mathematical languages.

Napell, Sondra, 1975. **TA Training Workshop.** Berkeley: University of California.

This booklet was designed to accompany a TA Training workshop at Berkeley. It acquaints the beginning teacher with a variety of teaching techniques and classroom formats which facilitate learning. It also discusses ways teachers can analyze and refine their teaching behaviors.

O'Neill, William F., 1981. **Educational Ideologies: Contemporary Expressions of Educational Philosophy.** California: Goodyear Publishing Company.

William O'Neill, from the University of Southern California, says that this book emerged out of an attempt to find new ways of thinking about the traditional approach to educational philosophies. The book is well-organized and proceeds from the more conservative and traditional ideologies to those which are more liberal and unconventional. He admits to his model being oversimplified and conceptual in nature, however, the book is a very useful outline of ideologies. Included is also an Educational Ideologies Inventory which is a test to determine your basic educational philosophy.

Passmore, John, 1980. **The Philosophy of Teaching.** Cambridge, MA: Harvard University, Press. 259 pages.

This book deals generally with the philosophies and concepts of teaching -- programmatically in the first two chapters and more specifically in the remainder of the book. It is useful as an overview.

Pause, M., 1976. **Teaching the Design Studio: A Case Study.** Cambridge: MIT, Ph.D. Thesis. 327 pages.

This Ph.D. Thesis begins with a historical summary of MIT's Department of Architecture, expanding on six case studies taken as representative of the period 1865-1974. Pause describes the changes occurring over time relative to design studio teaching. He discusses issues basic to teaching design studios and proposes a method of teaching design which emphasizes the teacher as a resource person in an environment of cooperative learning.

Posner, M. I., 1973. **Cognition, An Introduction.** Brighton, England: Scott, Foresman and Co. 208 pages.

Postman, Neil and Charles Weingartner, 1969. **Teaching as a Subversive Activity.** New York: Del Publishing. 219 pages.

A less current, but not necessarily less relevant, look at changing teaching methods and how to make education more relevant.

Postman, Neil, 1979. **Teaching as a Conserving Activity.** New York: Del Publishing. 224 pages.

Postman maintains that the function of education is to offer counter argument. Television is the first curriculum, school is the second. The book is full of good ideas including how TV and school should complement each other.

Pratt, Richard, 1977. **Ideology and Education.** New York: David McKay Co., Inc. 305 pages.

Rauh, Richard and David Wright, 1976. **Beginning Design Courses at Schools of Architecture in Western Europe.** Cambridge, MA: Harvard, Graduate School of Design. 798 pages.

Twenty introductory architecture courses in Europe are the basis of this report. An interesting resource of ideas, the paper notes the lack of information on establishing and presenting introductory design courses.

Ritter, Paul, 1966. **Educreation: Education for Creation, Growth and Change.** Oxford: Pergamon Press. 380 pages.

The general purposes of this book are to show that a new concept of education in architecture is required, in the opinion of the author, to demonstrate the new pattern in the context of educational theories, to indicate the general implications of the new concept and to show what ideas emerge from the new pattern of thinking. The concept of educreation is biased towards creation, growth, flexibility, adaptation and development. Ritter suggests that self-regulation should replace compulsion, cooperation should replace competition and a therapeutic attitude should replace moralist judgment.

Sargent, L. T., 1972. **Contemporary Political Ideologies.** Homewood, IL: Dorsey Press. 194 pages.

Schein, Edgard H., 1972. **Professional Education: Some New Directions.** New York: McGraw Hill. 163 pages.

This book gives an overview of professional education. The values and needs of students of professions are constantly changing as they advocate extending services to clients who have been historically underserved. Students are also demanding more flexible timing of their education and different pacing and organization of curriculums. Schein elaborates on the innovations he considers necessary for professional education and also describes a model of the processes of change itself.

Schon Donald and Chris Argyris, 1975. **Theories in Practice.** San Francisco: Jossey-Bass. 224 pages.

A discussion of theories of deterministic human behavior and their effects on learning, and subsequently practicing, a profession. The book refers to the important transition from an attitude which defies learning to one conducive to learning.

Sharan, Shlomo and Yael Sharan, 1976. **Small Group Teaching.** Englewood Cliffs, NJ: Educational Technology Publications. 237 pages.

Sheffield, Edward, 1974. **Teaching in the Universities: No One Way.** Montreal: McGill-Queen's University Press. 252 pages.

A collection of 23 essays written by Professors who were identified by their peers and students as being excellent educators. The papers are personal expressions of teaching, which agree upon three important notions: 1) the role of teachers is to stimulate students to become active learners on their own, 2) there is no one way to play the teacher's role, and 3) the importance of caring is emphasized.

Silberman, Charles E., 1970. **Crisis in the Classroom.** New York: Random House. 553 pages.

Simon, Herbert A., 1969. **The Sciences of the Artificial.** Cambridge, MA: MIT Press. 123 pages.

Stewart, Norman R., 1978. **Systematic Counseling.** Englewood Cliffs, NJ: Prentice-Hall Inc. 376 pages.

Travers, Robert M., 1982. **Essentials of Learning: The New Cognitive Learning for Students of Education.** New York: MacMillan Publishers. 570 pages.

This covers everything you would want to know about cognitive learning. It has excellent chapter summaries. The chapters, "Transfer Problem Solving" and "Motivation and Learning" are most useful.

Wales, C. E. and R. A. Stager, 1977. **Guided Design: Part I.** Morgantown: West Virginia University.

Weatherhead, Arthur C., 1941. **The History of Collegiate Education in Architecture in the United States.** Los Angeles, California: A Dissertation at Columbia University. 259 pages.

A doctoral dissertation at Columbia University, 1941, the study traces the development of collegiate education in architecture from its beginning in America through its important phases. The work is organized around three distinct periods: early, eclectic and modern. It is full of specific data on curriculum and statistics as well as concise summaries of the characteristics of certain schools and periods.

White, Jane N. and Collins W. Burnett, 1981. **Higher Education Literature: An Annotated Bibliography.** Phoenix, AZ: Oryz Press. 177 pages.

White, Stanley, 1953. **The Teaching of Landscape Architecture.** East Lansing, MI: NCILA Report. 97 pages.

This document is a "classic" on the teaching of landscape architecture. It is written in a handbook type style which includes aims and scope, background, systems, methods, content and facilities . . . full of ideas for teaching.

Whitehead, A. N., 1929. **The Aims of Education.** New York: New American Library. 247 pages.

Whitehead says that "one main idea runs through the various chapters: the students are alive, and the purpose of education is to stimulate and guide their self development." The corollary follows that teachers should also be alive with living thoughts. This book, written in 1929, is a protest against dead knowledge and inert ideas. The various chapters originated as lectures or addresses and span the years from 1912 to 1929. A classic book in terms of goals of education.

Wilson, John A. R., Mildred C. Roebeck and William B. Michael, 1974. **Psychological Foundations of Learning and Teaching.** New York: McGraw Hill. 589 pages.

This provides the tools to aid teachers in using learning and human development theory to help students become self-directing individuals. The book is clearly divided into chapters with good summaries. See **Short Cuts** (Chapter 2 **Ideabook**).

Wilson, Robert and Jeffy Gaff, 1975. **College Professors and Their Impact on Students.** New York: John Wiley and Sons. 220 pages.

What are the ways in which different faculty members influence or fail to influence different students? Studies to characterize both faculty and students were split into: Faculty views of teaching, and; Faculty impact on students. The chapter on Characteristics of Effective College Teachers is most interesting.

Wolman, Benjamin B., 1981. **Contemporary Theories and Systems in Psychology.** New York: Plenum Press 639 pages.

Young, R. E. (Editor), 1980. **Fostering Critical Thinking, New Directions for Teaching and Learning #3.** San Francisco: Jossey-Brass. 103 pages.

The purpose of this volume is to know more about critical thinking -- what it is, what influences it, what works and what does not in teaching and testing it. The book is developed to be of use to university teachers. The chapter by Robert Yinger on "Can We Really Teach Them to Think" and one by Jerry Stonewater on "Strategies for Problem Solving" are the most useful for design teachers.

journals

Abel, Chris, 1980. "Function of Tacit Knowledge in Learning to Design," **Design Studies,** Vol. 1, No. 2, pp. 208-214.

Archer, Bruce, 1979. "Design as a Discipline: Whatever Became of the Three R's," **Design Studies,** Vol. 1, No. 1, p. 17.

Barnett, Jonathan, 1970. "Studio Teaching is Out of Date," **Architectural Record,** Vol. 148, No. 4, p. 128.

Bender, Richard, 1979. "Operational Games in Architectural Design," **JAE,** Vol. 33, No. 1, pp. 2-6.

Bischoff, Ann L., 1979. **The Construct Validity of Creativity Measure.** CELA.

Bonta, Juan Pablo, 1979. "Simulation Games in Architectural Education," **JAE,** Vol. 31, No. 1, pp. 12-18.

Bosworth, F. S. and R. C. Jones, 1978. "Deja Vu: Excerpts from a Study of Architecture Schools," **JAE,** Vol. 31, No. 3, pp. 21-26.

Burnett, C. (Editor), 1975. "Pedagogical Ideas for Architectural Educations," **JAE,** AIA/ACSA Teachers Seminar Catalogue, Vol. 28, No. 1 and 2.

Collegiate Schools of Architecture, 1980. "Technics and Design Education," **JAE,** Vol. 33, No. 2.

Collins, P., 1955. "Architectural Education Two Hundred Years Ago," **RIBA Journal,** Vol. 62, No. 6, pp. 263-264.

Comerio, Mary C. and Jeffrey M. Chusid (Editors), 1982. **Proceedings of the 69th Annual Meeting of the Association of Collegiate Schools of Architecture.**

Cross, Anita, 1980. "Design and General Education," **Design Studies,** Vol. 1, No. 4, pp. 202-206.

Cuff, Dana, 1980. "Teaching and Learning Design Drawing," **JAE,** Vol. 33, No. 3, pp. 5-9.

Ellis, Russ, 1981. "The Social in the Studio," **JAE,** Vol. 34, No. 3, pp. 29-31.

Francis, Mark, 1982. "Behavioral Approaches and Issues in Landscape Architecture Education and Practice," **Landscape Journal,** Vol. 1, No. 2, pp. 92-95.

Green, C. W. B., 1971. "Learning to Design," **Architecture Research and Teaching**, Vol. 2, No. 1, pp. 40-46.

Hodges, Michael, 1978. **The Use of Affective Domain to Structure Performance Objectives for Landscape Architectural Courses.** NCILA.

Jukuri, Mary, 1978. **Creativity and Education.** NCILA.

Jules, Frederick A., 1974. "An Approach to Architectural Education," **JAE**, Vol. 26, No. 4, pp. 114-119.

Koberg, Don, 1978. "Presenting: Architects on Stage," **JAE**, Vol. 31, No. 4, pp. 8-12.

Koh, Jusuck, 1982. "Ecological Design: A Post Modern Design Paradigm of Holistic Philosophy and Evolutionary Ethic," **Landscape Journal**, Vol. 1, No. 2, pp. 76-84.

Kvashny, Alon, 1982. "Enhancing Creativity in Landscape Architectural Education," **Landscape Journal**, Vol. 1, No. 2, pp. 104-111.

Laurie, Michael, 1982. **Landscape Architecture in the Future.** Unpublished, San Francisco. Paper based on talk given to CSLA congress in Toronto.

Lifchez, Ray, 1974. "From Inside to Outside: A Journey to Architecture," **JAE**, Vol. 27, No. 1, pp. 27-36.

Lifchez, Ray, 1974. "Being There: Intentionality in Architecture," **JAE**, Vol. 27, No. 2 and 3, pp. 41-51.

Lifchez, Ray, 1976. "Notes on the Role of Criticism in Educating Future Architects," **JAE**, Vol. 29, No. 4, p. 4.

Lifchez, Ray, 1978. "Teaching a Social Perspective to Architecture Students," **JAE**, Vol. 31, No. 3, pp. 11-16.

Lifchez, Ray, 1981. "Students as Research Subjects: Conflicting Agendas in the Classroom," **JAE**, Vol. 34, No. 3, pp. 16-23.

Lowe, Jeremy B., 1970. "The Assessment of Students' Architectural Design Drawings," **Architectural Research and Teaching**, Vol. 1, No. 1, pp. 37-45.

Lydon, Donlyn, 1982. "Design: Inquiry and Implication," **JAE**, Vol. 35, No. 3, pp. 2-9.

Martin, L., 1970. "Education Around Architecture," **RIBA Journal**, Vol. 77, No. 9, pp. 398-402.

Maxwell, R., 1970. "Teaching and Learning," **RIBA Journal**, Vol. 77, No. 10, pp. 463-466.

Mayo, James, 1978. "Propaganda with Design: Environmental Dramaturgy in the Political Rally," **JAE**, Vol. 32, No. 2, pp. 27-30.

Porter, William, 1979. "Architecture Education in the University Context: Dilemmas and Directions," **JAE**, Vol. 32, No.3, pp. 3-7.

Rigterink, R., 1970. **SLATE: An Alternative Studio Method of Design Education.** NCILA.

Rittel, Horst, 1971. "Some Principles for the Design of an Educational System for Design," **JAE**, Vol. 25, No. 2 and 3, pp. 16-26.

Sand, Margaret Palm, 1975. **Advocacy Education: Out of the Need for Relevancy.** NCILA.

Simmons, Gordon, 1978. "Analogy in Design: Studio Teaching Models," **JAE**, Vol. 31, No. 3, pp. 18-20.

Stringer, Peter, 1970. "Architecture as Education," **RIBA Journal**, Vol. 77, No. 1, pp. 19-22.

Treib, Marc, 1982. "Of Cardboard Cities and Public Politics," **JAE**, Vol. 35, No. 3, pp. 18-21.

Whiffen, Marcus (Editor), 1964. "The Teaching of Architecture," **AIA-ACSA Teaching Seminar**, Cranbrook: Cranbrook Press. NA 2108-.A8.

Youtz, Philip N., 1966. "Ten Sources for Architectural Design," **AIA Journal**, Vol. 45, No. 2, pp. 43-43.

acknowledgments

The **Ideabook** has many authors. The numerous people I interviewed and talked to casually, join the names without faces, whose ideas I read in books and articles, as contributors to the **Ideabook.**

Thank you to the interviewees listed on the following page who donated their time and energy to the project.

Thank you to Tom Dickert and Clare Cooper Marcus from the Department of Landscape Architecture and Bob Wilson from Teaching Innovation and Evaluation Services (TIES) on the University of California, Berkeley campus, for their time, energy and support.

Thank you to the Landscape Architecture Foundation (LAF). Their research grant helped make more interviewees accessible and allowed for more computer time -- as did funding from the Beatrice Farrand Fund.

Thank you to the students of the Landscape Architecture Department at University of California, Berkeley with whom I have discussed teaching and learning. Their support and encouragement was invaluable.

Thank you to my colleagues at the University of British Columbia, Larry Diamond, Pat Miller and Doug Paterson, who are making my first teaching job so enjoyable.

Finally, a big thank you to my husband, David Fushtey, who gave me moral support and discussed format and philosophies with untiring patience.

interviewees

Russ Beatty: UC Berkeley: LANDSCAPE ARCHITECT

Eldon Beck: UC Berkeley: LANDSCALE ARCHITECT

Sam Davis: UC Berkeley: ARCHITECT

Frances Dean: Cal Poly Pomona: LANDSCAPE ARCHITECT

Kim Dovey: UC Berkeley: ARCHITECT

Tony Dubovsky: UC Berkeley: ARTIST

Mark Francis: UC Davis: LANDSCAPE ARCHITECT

Allan Gatzke: San Francisco: LANDSCAPE ARCHITECT/PLANNER

Randy Hester: UC Berkeley: LANDSCAPE ARCHITECT

Sara Ishikawa: UC Berkeley: ARCHITECT

Spiro Kostof: UC Berkeley: ARCHITECTURE HISTORIAN

Michael Laurie: UC Berkeley: LANDSCAPE ARCHITECT

Lars Lerup: UC Berkeley: ARCHITECT

Ray Lifchez: UC Berkeley: ARCHITECT

Clare Cooper Marcus: UC Berkeley: PLANNER

Joe McBride: UC Berkeley: FORESTER

Bob McGilvray: University of B.C.: ARCHITECT/LANDSCAPE ARCHITECT

Helge Olsen: UC Davis: FURNITURE DESIGNER

Doug Paterson: UC Berkeley: LANDSCAPE ARCHITECT

Joe Rodriguez: UC Berkeley: LANDSCAPE ARCHITECT

Alex Scordelis: UC Berkeley: ENGINEER

Gerald Smith: Cal Poly San Luis Obispo: LANDSCAPE ARCHITECT

Dale Sutliss: Cal Poly San Luis Obispo: LANDSCAPE ARCHITECT

Bob Tetlow: UC Berkeley: LANDSCAPE ARCHITECT

Robert Thayer: UC Davis: LANDSCAPE ARCHITECT

Marc Treib: UC Berkeley: ARCHITECT

Clyde Winters: San Francisco: DESIGNER

Mark von Wodtke: Cal Poly Pomona: LANDSCAPE ARCHITECT

Ortha Zebroski: Berkeley: LANDSCAPE ARCHITECT

about the author

Moura Quayle, Assistant Professor in the Landscape Architecture Program and the School of Architecture at the University of British Columbia, received the Bachelor of Landscape Architecture degree from the University of Guelph in 1974. She completed the Master of Landscape Architecture degree at the University of California, Berkeley in 1983 with a research emphasis on design education. Between her two degrees Ms. Quayle was a site planner for British Columbia Provincial Parks, had her own practice for 5 years in Victoria, B.C. and then worked for an interdisciplinary firm of architects, planners and landscape architects in Montreal. She was President of the B.C. Society of Landscape Architects (1979-80) and Secretary of the Canadian Society of Landscape Architects (1980-81).

She was awarded a Landscape Architecture Foundation research scholarship for Masters work on design education and received the ASLA Award of Honor in 1983 for work at University of California, Berkeley.

In July 1983, Ms. Quayle joined the faculty of the University of British Columbia in a joint teaching appointment between Landscape Architecture and Architecture. She has subsequently received a Canada Council grant to investigate computer-aided participatory design. Other research activities involve exploring connections between general learning theories and specific design learning, public environmental education methods and cultural landscape indicators of landscape changes.

index